Diaries of a Young Mystic

Lucy Oliver

Published by Lucy Oliver, 2024.

DIARIES OF A YOUNG MYSTIC

First edition. March 27, 2024.

ISBN: 979-8224268894

Written by Lucy Oliver.

Table of Contents

To the reader:

Tread softly through these pages, and allow your heart to speak where it finds a resonance. This is the way of those who search in common life for what is real and lasting.

Also by Lucy Oliver

The Meditator's Guidebook ISBN *0-89281-360*-1 Destiny, Inner Traditions USA 1991, re-printed from *Meditation and the Creative Imperative* Dryad Press, ISBN 0 8521 9698 9 London 1987, and in German translation *Meine Insel der Stille I*SBN 3-89304-141-9. Volkar-Magnum 1996

Tessellations: Patterns of Life and Death in the Company of a **Master** ISBN 978 183859 294 3 Matador UK 2020

https://www.meaningbydesign.co.uk/

PREFACE

———

These diaries are a first-hand, intimate record of soul-search and growth through the eyes of a young woman living and studying in the university town of Oxford in the late 1970's.

The woman was my younger self.

Fifty years later, at the age of 72, I found the forgotten diaries, and was moved to discover in their pages not only a poetic evocation of the 'town of dreaming spires', but a fresh and insightful chronicle of youth, love and the quest for wisdom. I have added some narrative background and commentary informed by the hindsight and perspective of a further half-century of living, so the resulting book is an interwoven reflection from two perspectives: Youth and Age.

My path was a combination of academic study and direct perception, initially supported by art, literature and poetry, but ultimately finding direction by means of esoteric philosophy. The six years of diaries represent an intense maturing process. As I read my own words from long ago, I was immersed again in the mellow beauty of the ancient university town which was for me a stage both for delight and intimate reflection at the pageant of life, and for love, loss, reversals, despair and struggle.

I began by living an Oxford idyll, but a crack arose in the porcelain of my experience, a crack which nearly swallowed me. The person who emerged from it was new, and wiser.

INTRODUCTION

―――――

I n my seventh decade of life, I opened a small tin trunk which had been stored under the stairs for ever so long. In it I found some battered exercise books, the diaries I had written devotedly from late childhood until a transitional moment at the age of 29 when the writing suddenly stopped. The oldest book was carefully covered in brown paper, as if to conceal its identity, but the latest, 1979, bore an Oxford University crest on its faded blue cover.

Pulled by some deep-seated impulse to explore fresh fields, after university and beginning a teaching career, at the age of 22 I left my childhood, my career, my much-loved family and homeland in Australia for the other side of the world. I am still here, far away from those beginnings.

For many young people, their 'twenties' are characteristically turbulent years, full of experiments, experiences, failures and successes, all part of a quest for a firm identity and role in life. I had a clear inner trajectory which could be characterized as searching for 'Meaning', 'ultimate meaning', or 'God' (though I was wary of dogma and received ideas).

Essentially, I was looking for those intimations of experience beyond the personal, like ripples on a pond from some yet invisible subterranean activity. Without other guidance at that point, by writing the diaries I had a sounding-board, an on-going dialogue with self. It was part of a process of fashioning a reasonably coherent worldview and identity.

DIARIES OF A YOUNG MYSTIC

After half a century of living on from those dates, I can see in them repeated patterns of expectation and behaviour of which, naturally, I had been oblivious at the time. What interests me now, is the drive behind these patterns. In the words of Dylan Thomas: "The force that through the green fuse drives the flower, Drives my green age....". These were the years of exploring my "green fuse", and just as a fuse is designed to do, it broke when the current was too strong.

I sought for illumination through beauty, the arts, atmosphere and spirit of place, and through friendships and lovers. All these were avenues for refining the understanding of Love, which, at the grand age of twenty in an earlier diary, I had pronounced was my 'goal in life'. I surmised it was a transformative kind of process, and expected that it would take time and experimentation. After all, I was aiming at what seemed to me to be the 'Highest', but what name should I give to it—God? Nature? Beauty? Relationship? Wisdom? Peace? In the event, I just collected whatever experiences came my way, and mulled over them to see what evolved.

'Love' is a large aspiration. The word denotes everything from the sublime and sacred, to the epitome of vulgarity and predation, and every shade in between. Religion, psychology, literature and popular culture offer quite different yardsticks. When a deep connection is made and broken, it can cross all those boundaries.

One thing I have noted, in the lives of others as well as in myself, is how from mid-life onwards something vital in one's being and aspiration can wane with the dulling round of fulfilling expectations, of repeating the same message, and of tending to the limitless needs of others. Opening my old diaries had the effect for me of re-connecting with some kind of inner force, like a seed in my Being, which age had buried under an accumulation of life-experience. It was salutary for me now to sense again this wellspring, a central, primal drive, the 'force' behind the 'green fuse'. All the other impulsions and cross-currents which have led me to this point are not of this wellspring and force. It is beyond the personal.

I have the good fortune of an active healthy Seventies, and most of my earlier preoccupations or obsessions are gone. Both the external and internal environment are more settled. Ambition was never part of my make-up, for career, fame, recognition, success or any of the usual drivers, so the absence of them makes no difference. That may sound passive, but only if the pursuit of grasping what the world offers is the benchmark. All the great spiritual traditions are extremely clear in reiterating that they are not!

It has taken me seventy years to realize what I have heard so many times: that the soul, or essence, or consciousness is pristine, and is not the same as the identifications, quirks and characteristics we know as 'me'. I lived *from* it in my youth, but like everyone, I was well ensnared in reactions to external and internal events. As I read now, I can see this entanglement, but I can also see a push from within, like a shadowy alter-ego, quietly dictating my decisions and contributing flickers of light which—just sometimes—I caught and recorded in my writing, even though I hadn't recognised, named or identified it.

I wanted very much to follow these intimations, but it was still a lightbulb moment when I realised that there was a way of *ordering* these scattered intimations into a structured whole which allowed for evolution. Order is a creative force. A pile of bricks becomes a house when they are organised according to the principles of house-creation, utilising the laws of space and form to realise an aim and design. Intimations need the same treatment if they are to house the spirit. It is not enough just to *sense* things, and even less productive just to *believe* things.

The diaries ceased suddenly in 1979, when my life took a different turn. I was surprised to see how abruptly my writing habit terminated at the age of 29 when I entered into marriage and motherhood. Was I too busy to write anymore? Maybe. But also, the concerns with which I had wrestled, shared and worked out through writing in my journals had changed. I had entered the period of interior work and training, exploring systematically the principles of order through esoteric study, practice and meditation under guidance which I have described in my book *Tessellations: Patterns of Life and Death in the Company of a Master.*

Keeping a journal is by nature self-referential. On the one hand, it allows for reflection by creating a bit of distance from circumstances, and fosters insight, but the downside is self-confirmation which ultimately can inhibit further growth. The sly edge of self-justification is difficult to avoid, and a personal echo-chamber can insidiously solidify into a platform for re-asserting one's opinions rather than uncovering fresh insight. As my horizons expanded, it began to feel like an indulgence to focus on myself as before.

Therefore, I abandoned my mute confidant.

In transcribing the diaries, it is my hope that many, young or old, will recognise in themselves the voice of this young woman embarking on life, a time when everything is new and filled with inchoate promise, and perhaps be prompted into a personal exercise in the 'getting of wisdom'.

―――――――――――

DIARIES OF A YOUNG MYSTIC

<u>Note</u>

Except for family or public figures, the friends who pass in and out of this narrative will be designated by initials only. Though it is unlikely any will stumble across this account, names are powerful, and I do not feel I have the right to pronounce their names and drag their essence into my world. I will be consistent in my use of initials, changing as appropriate if duplicated, but for me, the initial will evoke their presence.

<u>Disclaimer</u>

The views and judgements expressed either in the diaries or in the commentary are personal to my experience, and are not intended as advice, nor judgement of others, nor to represent any theoretical approach to any issues raised.

PRELUDE
A Meeting with Myself

———

I watch her standing there. Her face is softer now, the lines of age blurring the features once so sharp and clear. She is gazing across the canyon waiting for the dawn, next to a small tree clinging precipitously to the edge. The tree is gnarled, having withstood the force of wind, snow and burning sun for many generations. They are alike, the woman and the tree.

In the far distance a horizontal line of red and gold appears as the rocks take up the dawn and begin to glow. It is happening yet again, another morning on the earth at its most magnificent, and as I watch, her face is burnished with the rising sun, and now I see four women, each alive with questioning.

I see a chubby child in dungarees, hardly taller than the long stem of grass which tickles her chin, and she is laughing at the grass and at the world which is so fresh and unknown. There will be a lot to discover.

I see a young woman with large grey eyes, courted by this man and that, who find her intriguing and beautiful. It's a wild ride for the young, and she is resolved to follow every thread back to its source and to know wherefrom such richness and folly originate.

Then a matron rests quietly on the rocks. She has seen her children grow, she has read and pondered and wondered, but she has also worked the threads, diligently, not knowing where they might lead, and accepted the interweaving of sorrow as a gift of knowledge.

Her aged face is now as craggy as the earth, her body thin, but she and the sun are vital this morning and every morning, knowing that light replaces darkness and darkness replaces light. On these wheels the Ancient of Days is a traveller whom those who seek shall find.

Aroused by the flight of an eagle across my line of vision, I know I must seize the opportunity and ask of her the questions I've never had courage to ask:

How is it you are standing here? What have you done? What guided you? Can you give me even some clues as to what you've found which is truly important?

There are more questions jostling in my mind, but that's enough for now. She looks at me, not quite benevolently, but more with an air of appraisal. With a tiny touch of belligerence, because I am a genuine seeker, I lock my gaze onto her eyes. It is a mistake. Suddenly I am drawn in to a vast space, a darkness which is boundless, and my questions are like mere sparks in the depths of infinity. Time to row back.

She smiled then, and the crinkles are reassuringly human.

"I'll tell you", she said...........

CHAPTER 1
Oxford Beginnings

———

From August 1973 I settled in Oxford, not to study yet, but just as a suitable town to make a home after arriving in the UK from Australia the previous January. I had spent some time interacting with friends in Cambridge, travelling in Europe and had been living with my sister in London.

I arrived in Oxford with one suitcase and found accommodation in a small and lurid bed-sitting room along the Iffley Road. The hallway smelled of cabbage, but my little back room looked out onto a gnarled crab-apple tree with steps down to the garden, so I was content to perch here for my early months. I knew no one. I took on work at a bookshop in the Broad, and explored the town and its environs, gradually establishing friendships, including the one which had such major impact on determining the course of the rest of my life.

I was 22 years old.

Friday 3rd August 1973.

Oxford. The beginning.

A bare beginning; I feel absolutely empty: of future, of present even.

This evening as I walked down Meadow Lane by the river my mind wandered vaguely around the borders of what I have, and could go no further. It was cool, the grass wet, the sky tumbled and suffused with Turneresque light over the low river trees. Not a comforting environment.

I don't know Oxford yet, nor love it. I am simply here. Pure unaccommodated Lucy! There is almost something pure about this loneliness, the dull clang of my thoughts, the hungry look with which I follow people talking or walking together. I suspect it is a temporary state, that somehow a future will form. I just can't see it now.

The ache left by the affair with S. No happiness in the memories; just sadness and emptiness. Always at the back of my thoughts is knowing he leaves tomorrow, without relation to me, as if we had never met.

This was the aftermath of a bitter-sweet interlude of falling in love on a bridge in the moonlight by Rydal Water in the Lake District, where I had joined new friends on a Cambridge retreat course. The brief love affair was never destined to last: I was still an itinerant, he deeply embedded in Cambridge life and studies, and about to embark on a career abroad. Our paths crossed and parted, but I still recall the lovely light in his clear grey eyes.

Sunday 5th August 1973

Oh nasty, nasty day! I watched the rain falling steadily on the sodden garden without my window. This garden is palling on me! I think I'd rather a busy street corner with hurrying people and swishing cars than this silent dripping. And now I hear the wind swirling in all the trees.

Still, I stirred myself from *Lucky Jim (a novel by Kingsley Amis)* to go out about five. (Amusing book; I enjoyed its cheeky desperation and feel oddly comforted.)

Evensong in Christchurch, though well sung, somehow suggested to me both a cattle-market and a school speech night—something about the formalism and pomposity, with visitors in rustling windcheaters gawking at unfamiliar pious booklets, trying to take in windows, choir, ceremony, neighbours and God all at once.

But I had a lovely walk around Christchurch Meadow and Merton. The rain fell mistily and there were no people. It was very beautiful; the towers across the field, thick gardens blazing with colour even in the rain. A cluster of roses leant on an old dark wall; the cobbles shone in narrow streets where, blessedly, gorgeously, no tourists toured!

Just me, and the streets. Me jumping puddles, defending my red umbrella from the marauding wind, and hearing the bells at six o'clock—Christchurch deep, Merton chiming lyrically, Magdalen distant.

First impressions! Later the many evensongs of Oxford became for me a precious resource.

Wednesday 15th August 1973

'Write', I say. Write what?

Write about the empty streets of Oxford, full with sun on yellow stone, and the warm air of summer. Write about the lime-sun under the trees of Magdalen deer-park, as it was this evening through the bars of the black gate, and the tottering, flicking deer. The scene filled me with distance: time-distance, Merrie England and stories of the past. The bend of the river, thick as oil and still, by Christchurch Meadow.

Write about the streaming, clattering impressions of Parkers Bookshop as I move among the shelves of book-carcasses, compelling but unable to seize me as I flutter from tin to table to paper to coffee cup to one-dimensional strangers. At 5.30 I leave work.

The empty streets; the empty evening of my mind and body, with all emotions hibernating it seems.

The orange and purple ritualized silence of my bed-sit, and the sleeping, breathing, eating, fiddling functions which take place in its musty air.

So! Life in Oxford!

There is, however, another little life running parallel, very insubstantial, made of the sort of stuff dreams are made on, to be reduced by a breath of fog. There in dreams at night—very clear, simple lucid dreams, and thoughts of past and people. This barely existing 'life' has not even a nodding acquaintance with rationality or conscious myth-making, and somehow, I am afraid of it, in case it solidifies because there is nothing else solid in my life.

I keep expecting things to change. I wonder...

Thursday 16th August 1973

Heatwave! And I have found a perfect place to spend a summer afternoon. There is not an ingredient missing as I am bounced about on the top of a red bus through countryside to Boar's Hill. I walked down a shady road, turned into a wood and followed a little path through blackberries. And suddenly—lo! The path burst out into a field of wheat, yellow in the heat. Beyond the fields of green hedges and trees, and shimmering in the distance are the 'dreaming' towers of Oxford. Shades of Matthew Arnold indeed!

So now I am cross-legged in soft grass under a clump of trees so artistic that I suspect them of being stage-props, as I survey this rural kingdom. It is a spot where great thoughts are called for. I have none at present, but I am wondering back into past summers, where who knows what young people may have come to watch the ripening wheat and feel its symbolism, and then is forgotten through age, or accomplishment, and death of the dreaming-mind.

Yea, it moves me, even with the breeze in my long dress, to know I am one of such a long circle, or a fibre in a long plait. Where does it end? I am following so many; will be followed by so many; but none are Me, and we have no contact.

Sunday 19th August 1973

Warm Sunday by the river and wandering around Iffley village. I was rudely put to flight by cows, as I lay on the bank watching launches wash past. At my first awareness of fierce breathings and lumbering munches, I hurriedly seized my sandals and literally hopped down the tow-path. One leg had gone profoundly to sleep, but I heard ominous lowing close behind, and a great black and white head appeared through the hedge. I rather like cows, but they are too big and unpredictable to have them wandering near me.

Also, perhaps I associate them with death—their big dumb heads turn into bleached skulls on desert sands, horns and black eye-sockets—an ancient and terrifying symbol of evil.

Anyway, they assumed their beautiful form (distant!) later, as I sat through the evening hours by Merton wall. The playing field hopped with birds, and two large worms bit the dust, disappearing behind the bright eyes of a thrush and blackbird. I couldn't associate any "first, fine careless rapture" with this particular thrush as he watched me out of one eye and contemplated the gastronomic wriggling from within his speckled stomach.

In Christchurch Meadow the cows moved softly across a background of milky trees. With each bell-sounding, the mists grew thicker.

I was meditating on the last few pages of Huxley's *Eyeless in Gaza*, and on the unity of all life. "The substance of frenzy is the same as the substance of peace".

And a passage which spoke to me:

"'Death", said Mark Staithes. "It's the only thing we haven't succeeded in completely vulgarizing." Huxley continues with a metaphor of dogs lifting their legs against art, religion, heroism and love, thereby defiling them with their 'visiting-cards'.

"But death remains out of reach...faithful...if we choose to risk our lives, we can risk them as completely as ever we did."

Death is the only absolute I can see, as life is so chameleon and confusing in its manifestations. Only death can I be sure of achieving. When there is nothing else, death can be an inspiration to live on, the sole certainty which no man, god or fate can take away or tamper with. It makes me feel like a tramp with one glittering possession, beside which all the buffetings and incidents of life on the road seem merely incidental, by-the-by.

For the gift of Death, for the grace of this commonality, this communion with every other human being throughout time, I want to live totally, rejoicingly, constructively, healingly and lovingly, so as to transfigure Death into affirmation, completion and transcendence of Life. It seems to me that at the moment of Death, Life triumphs and is affirmed—if one has the awareness that death is a condition of life, just as transience is a condition of beauty.

It could be said that these sentiments returned to haunt me a couple of years later when I seriously considered taking the 'gift', and realised that a gift is, by definition, not to be forcibly grabbed at will. A gift is given, not taken.

Also, I'm pondering the 7 sides of any question. That is, no question has 'sides', merely facets, like a diamond. Which makes its outlines difficult to fully grasp, as it sends off lights in all directions. Nearly all questions, considered properly, do this.

Illusions can have a role too. The half-sight of an unusual configuration of gravel by the wall of Merton College earlier produced an illusion of shadow by the wall and sunshine beyond. I felt quite uplifted, even though there was no actual sun to cast a shadow! This made me think that if the illusion of sun can be created and is sufficient to produce a psychological effect, should we not work at creating such illusions sometimes?

DIARIES OF A YOUNG MYSTIC

Friday 24th August 1973

It's been a fine day!

As it was my Day-off, I set off early with books and lunch to commence a river walk at Folly Bridge. It was industrial until Osney Lock, where Chaucer set the Miller's Tale. I could see no Chaucerian signs, yet it delighted me: the green waters, the sparkling and flowered lock and cottage (best kept lock on the Thames!); the old streets of houses, blank-faced, but lent grace by the magnificent row of trees by the river side.

There a woman with dyed hair sunned her bunions, and ate chips with delicate relish.

The next delight was Bossom's boat-yard. Irresistibly reminded of France and M. Hulot (the dappled watery quality of some scene from 'Traffic'?) I stood and listened to the squawking of the geese and ducks across the flat pond. Herds of cows wandered into the water from Port Meadow; the boats shone, stacked in the sun and shadows of the leafy bank. It was midday, and joyously peaceful.

Then on to Binsey. Here I was lured from the tow-path by a tiny huddle of buildings and thatch. A winding road led past the cottages and into countryside so perfect, I smiled and swung my bags as I wandered barefoot down the lane. At the end, Binsey Church.

At this little Church, I spent several hours. How can I describe its loveliness? Entry through a wicket gate, and path along which Henry VIII and Catherine of Aragon must have come on their pilgrimage to the well of St Margaret. I sat against an ancient illegible stone and tried again to understand, to give some form to the emotion which buildings create: the interplay of mass and line; the way the porch in its simplicity fits snugly into the wall; above the double bell-tower through the yew tree. If only my mind were in working order!

Inside I had one of those rare experiences: the meeting with something which is perfect, which seems made of the same substance as oneself, leading to the sensation of perfect accord. I am sitting in a corner of this 13th century treasure, by the wooden pulpit where the sun streamed in through deeply inset windows and moved quietly with the motion of the trees without. The light was old; the atmosphere unmistakeably medieval. My eye is focused on an object above the pulpit, in the window light. An angel is there, caught in a moment of complete communion with his lute. It is of bronze I think, like a fire-screen, lightly sculptured and thrown into relief, and painted in muted browns, blue and gold.

Is it a good work of art? Who produced it? I do not know. It is there, and as long as it is there, I will come and sit before it.

I spent a long time trying to capture it on paper. The fluidity, the poise and balance of it—diagonal, a breath-suspending tension. Marvellous expression on the face, not coy or angelic, not falsely enraptured, not classically beautiful, but *listening*. Sensitive, intelligent, and self-effacing. The lute is the centre: the music one almost hears; the face one sees last of all. All is tossed, yet it breathes peace.

I now know it was an old bronze relief of the famous and much reproduced 'Angel with lute' by the renaissance painter Melozzo da Forli. Sadly, it is no longer there.

Thursday 30th August 1973

Reading Yehudi Menuhin's *Theme and Variations*. Another whom I deeply admire, and with whose attitude towards and understanding of life I feel in sympathy. How powerful actually is the effect of such men of wisdom, balance and beauty? How far do they combat prejudice, violence, fanaticism, bigotry, ignorance, hatred and the rest? Is it that there are fewer men of understanding than there are bigots? Or is the concentration and distortion of negative extremes a more powerful force in the universe?

I wish I could meet such a man for a teacher. I need one so much, for the closer I come to moments of serenity and insight, the clearer and clearer and CLEARER become the faults which stand hard and brittle like rocks in a sea, obstructing, diverting, threatening always to build up and increase their mass.

Yehudi Menuhin's face is of such beauty, like a face I have known before, or have always known. (Life before life?) His face is familiar, as if I know every line and fold. Why? Why has every face which has ever attracted me in a special way been similar? Like some archetypal face which I carry within me, their appeal must lie in the suggestion of familiarity. From whence cometh this archetypal face?

Is it an argument for reincarnation? Given we all have the same short lifespan, how can differences in Being be accounted for? Does it mean Man A has had more *quantity* (lives) of the appropriate *quality* to evolve in than Man B? How can one child at the age of 4 or 5 be aware of all kinds of truths, feel universal currents, childishly wrestle with good and evil, while another at the same tender age is quite unaware of these kind of dimensions to the universe, and might always remain so?

I was thinking the other day, that in my own little way, there were things I knew from the beginning that I could not possibly have acquired from any external source, family or books (especially before I could read!). How come? Certain reactions and attitudes which came instinctively, particularly when dealing with other people, which I just 'knew'. It's puzzling and provoking.

Could the development of an individual be determined in the beginning by certain metaphysical laws? We can measure scientific laws, but it's more reasonable here to assume the existence of laws of a different nature, like interdependence and inter-relationship, reciprocal and mutual forces, and balance.

I was on to something here with the intuition of metaphysical laws, though at this stage I had no knowledge of what they might be. But archetypal intimations and the intriguing idea of reincarnation, even though usually understood very simplistically without deeper thought and experience, are the beginning of an awareness of the bigger cycles of our existence.

I'm learning a lot at Parkers (*Bookshop*), oddly enough.

A scene: there's a small boy in my desk chair reading a book. I am filing through a drawer, vaguely aware that someone is sitting where I like to sit. Instead of simply vacating the chair, he turned a dazzling smile and bright eyes upon me: "I guess you'd like to sit down!" he said getting up. An answering smile from me as I sat down, and a lovely moment of communication ensued!

Such a variety of people you meet working here, and the chance to develop certain qualities previously rather meagre in me: like patience, and the immediate effect of oneself on another self.

I'm very garrulous tonight! With my discount I bought the Visconti Hours, expensively, but so rich and exquisite. It has made me see the world in miniature: vignettes of experience are jewel-like, and bordered within a period of time. At the moment, when I am walking around, scenes suddenly *crystallize*. Colours glow; every sense, not just visual, is simultaneously apprehended and extended in time, a feature particularly noticeable in a place like Oxford. Every scene has a historical past and is part of a continuing tradition, which is why it feels 'bordered'. I know that in a moment I will turn away, like turning the pages of a book, and move on to another scene, each frozen in perpetual stasis and movement.

This applies also to memories, detached at the moment of apprehension, yet involved, for as well as being an actor in the remembered scene, I am doing the seeing *then* and *now*.

Friday 31st August 1973

Australian poetry anthology. All the best of Australia is here, in the voices of its poets. All the poems I used to read and love as a child – how they recall a rhythm deep within me. Music may have its rhythm, so does poetry, perhaps even more so, as it gives expression to the inarticulate grounds of being, but speaks with an articulate voice. I hear Australia very clearly, and move with it.

Even in the bastion of Melbourne Uni's English department's 'rotting' creativity, the descriptions move me with an enormous nostalgia. The Old Arts Building: I know just exactly how the late winter's afternoon sun creeps under the arches and "greens the cabinets" in Prof. B's room. And the students- people I knew – so tellingly captured. I wish C and I had had more to say to each other, but we never would really, even if he had met 'me' instead of my image. What a strange interlude that was! He saw me through his poet's eyes, as an artist loving form – I was a sort of Chinese vase! And of course, a little mist of alcohol did wonders for the contours! I wonder if things are better for him now.

I was rather guileless in dealing with the attentions of a couple of senior lecturers who took an interest (a fancy) to me at the time. However, I was wary, wisely, and though flattered, and a little bit naïve, I maintained a certain distance.

H went further than his image of me, but he moulded me into his lines. I often think of H – not sure why. With affection though. I miss his affection, and wish that I had treated him better so we could still be friends. He was a fine man in many ways, and I shall treasure him.

Oh, how I reminisce! Must not read Australian poetry! I sound like an old woman writing her memoires!

CHAPTER 2
Poets and Choristers

———

Saturday 1st September 1973. Wales trip.

I have found a 'soul-mate' in this country of Wales. It has rained all day; visibility was nil; I battled with umbrella and wind and no buses, and yet I can say Wales is a fine place! What weird charm has it, that even the hideous discomforts I mention do not daunt my spirit?

At last I understand "in the cup of the vales"; "farmhouse in a fold of fields"; "the river-wended vales", etc. *(Dylan Thomas)* The country is all folded round its buildings and tiny towns, all of which seem to be climbing out of some nook and cranny of the land. It smells different. Carmarthen struck me as very different from an English town, more European, somehow allowing for more variety and contrasts (not so many of those rows and rows of wretched bow-windowed houses.)

And Dylan Thomas, of course.

I hear him everywhere, that poet who has become so much part of me and my way of looking at the world that I sometimes forget that I did not write the poems. He, of course, has made and shaped my vision.

Tonight, at St David's I sat on the Cathedral wall (14th C) to dine on fish and chips. A black dog befriended me, and breathed lovingly over my shoulder as I ate, watching each soggy morsel travel from the newspaper to my mouth. The love-affair ended on the instant the last greasy delicacy disappeared into my face.

But the scene before me merited even more involvement than the chips. What a moment when I first saw the cathedral, square and black with wetness, as the clouds lifted and rooks screamed and circled round the tower.

Later, sitting on the old wall, the sun was setting behind its massy-ness, and after all the rain, the evening shone. A glow rose over the fields and transfigured the house fronts, as the sky behind brooded in purple. A magnificent sunset! The landscape here has menace and an untamed quality I've not felt in England. It thrills me.

Sunday 2nd September 1973

Today I heard bells pealing for twenty minutes across the misty valley and reverberating in a stone tower. Seven people stood in a circle and pulled at the great ropes.

I walked most of the day round the windy coast and up hedged lanes. The afternoon sun saw me sitting on a rock by the road-side under my red umbrella, reading Dylan Thomas. I realized when a car went past what an eccentric figure I must appear sometimes, though I fondly believe I am invisible. Experience should teach me that, on the contrary, I tend to be noticed.

Ah well! I'm doing what comes naturally!

Monday 3rd September 1973 Laugharne—home of Dylan Thomas

DIARIES OF A YOUNG MYSTIC

Today I made my pilgrimage to Laugharne, and wandered alone, encountering nobody.

To my delight, there is very little Dylan-cult here (guess they couldn't stand him when he was alive!). His grave is a simple white cross in the midst of others. No sign, and not even a path worn to it. I found it purely by instinct, and was deeply moved by it – eloquent and fitting for the "black spit in the chapel fold", who had no great faith in the "religious wind".

Nothing anywhere is labelled or sign-posted.

I wandered along a flat path beside the mist-wreathed estuary. A horse browsed, birds cried, and I came upon the Boathouse on the rocky edge by climbing a path up the cliff, and there squatted the shed where he wrote. Through a large crack above the round door, everything appeared just as if he had left it a year or two ago. I could hardly believe it is twenty years since he left it to die in America.

Twenty years! I think of him as contemporary with me— yet already I am thinking in twenty-year periods. How old am I growing, and how fast!

A cob-webbed, unpainted table by the window, two broken chairs, an empty bookcase and an old heater. And of course, the grey view. This is where those "sawn, splay sounds" were put together, where the "moonshine-drinking Noah of the bay" built his ark. I sat on a bench and read the words over.

Then I went down onto the mud when the tide was low, where he hurled his poems after a quarrel with Caitlin, who got up before the tide next morning to retrieve his scattered and bedraggled works.

I could imagine this curving bay with the sun sparkling in the morning, and "salmon" with the setting sun, and wished I could see it thus. Particularly as I climbed Sir John's Hill and the hill above Milk Wood, I wished all was more "summery on the hill's shoulder". But imagination must serve until the event of a lengthier visit.

It is not Dylan, the man, whom I sought in this place, but Dylan the poet. Not a sentimental re-creation, but a pathway to the innermost lining of the poems which have shaped my life with their lyricism. And I found it there, and felt the words move in me and be born again. I will hug the memory of this day to my heart, a precious experience, and totally possessed. It cannot be undone; only time and the world can take the thrill off it, like the mud from my shoes, and the immediacy, leaving just a dot in the vast time-distance.

And the town will change, the shed be ruined or museum-ed; only the words endure.

But I have seen!

Saturday 15th September 1973

I think of all the people I have known and know. How round and real each one is; how they play across my memory; how I wish I could capture each one or blend them together into the marvellous tapestry they would make, seen from above, as it were! Not rendered still and gem-like, but seen moving within the limits of his or her life, and all these lives on a vast moving canvas.

I am another of these lives. It would mean transcending myself for this sort of vision!

I wish sometimes I were God, and could love all these people in their totality; just love them. But I'm not! I'm down here, eye to eye, and see only the side which is evident at the time: the irritating one, the one I enjoy, followed by the one which evokes no response in me. While I am part and sharer of it all, there are currents, frictions, affections and inter-rubbings.

Then – zap! I am God, and all sides exist at once! No inter-rubbings, just the still unified centre of loving in which all are one.

We are all, then, God.....?

People past, present, future, all separate and all one.

Sunday 16th September 1973

I feel at home everywhere because I love the world so much. But also nowhere, because sometimes it is so strange, this planet, so briefly and imperfectly known. (Can it be 'known' in the biblical sense?)

This afternoon. That cobweb in the sunshine. The little brown frog on my fingers, so soft and wet. The cress-full stream.

All being so complete. Even myself being whole and undemanding, because there is nothing to demand. Unself-conscious because I am not apart, not the object of any universal 'eye'. My limbs feel a part of me and the grass together.

Perhaps the proper use of the intellect is its overshadowing. Then, something which was becoming a little wizened with knowing too much, becomes young again.

How wonderful to want nothing! How beautiful it all is, all so full of form and presence!

Tuesday 25th September 1973

I do not want to be 'bought' by men. Because he takes her out, (she couldn't think of an excuse quick enough!) spends money on her entertainment, he therefore expects certain satisfactions in return. Why should he?

These meditations arise from my having left a disgruntled B at the bus-stop, having engineered a no-return to the college as he might have expected. But I felt guilty, not only because of his financing, and that I agreed to the 'date' (hate the word!) with reluctance anyway, foreseeing the outcome, but because there is a shady part of me which is almost prepared to see such reciprocity as a reasonable favour to another human being, fellow citizen etc.

Yet I don't feel prepared to offer myself as a trade-off while there remains the far better possibility of a relationship involving emotional commitment and the whole personality. Maybe when I'm 35 and still unmarried, I'll have given up the hope and be ready to clutch at straws!

Sunday 1st October 1973

Autumn fires and chestnuts and a strong freezing wind made the warmth of summer just a haunting memory, and the huddled visions of pinched and wrapped people in an all-pervading cold rose up again. This bitter England! This England of old people freezing in their homes, and narrow people shrinking into their overcoats!

But earlier today it was Lovely England. AW (*a recently made friend, distressed by a broken engagement*) called into the shop at closing time, looking wan, and carried me off. As we drove to his family home, the sun set brilliantly, clear and gold-leaf across the green tossed fields. No crops now – just furrows and grass. But it was simply lovely countryside of chestnut roads and small villages. His own village is perfect and the house likewise – rambling beams in a maze of rooms full of character, warmth, taste and beauty. They are a naval family.

A and I have a very strange relationship, and I'm sure there would never have been one but for his present state of great upset and trouble as he and his fiancée ran aground. I was a maternal breast and confiding ear at Parkers. The Rock again! I may help just by being, and thus restoring some balance to his vision of women, opening the possibility that there may be other women to fill the gap.

I like his lucidity, articulateness and self-knowledge. Strictly platonic: I will be most interested to see if it can work. Interesting to see how sex creates enormous complications and seems unavoidable, just by one being male and one female.

Discovered the I Ching. Beautiful, and above all, extra-ordinary. Consulted it about A and me as a test case, and was staggered at the resultant analysis and advice. Somehow, I have to cling to the advice because I can see very clearly how right it is.

LUCY OLIVER

Saturday 13th October 1973

The character of Oxford has certainly changed over the last week. From sunshine and foreigners, a sort of spread-out and characterless place, it has filled with young faces and scarves, people who belong here thronging the streets and laughing against the cold wintry wind as they gaze open-eyed at this city of cities.

There is something time-honoured about this new crop of freshers, like a cycle of nature, they flow into the city generation after generation to make it their own for a brief space of time. Then out into the world; their names flash in the newspapers, are bandied about in the arts, sciences, academic world; and then it is over. Except for the few—oblivion. But still they come, year after year, and there is no hint of this oblivion in their faces as they fumble with an unfamiliar cheque-book buying up their first load of text-books in the bookshop.

Thursday 18th October 1973

Autumn settles in with cold, sunny days and falling leaves. (The usual stuff etc.) And I'm starting to love this Oxford. How has it changed so, from bland beauty into deep graciousness? In the evenings the windows glow with a thousand warm centres of activity. The buildings at last are inhabited!

Went to Evensong at New College and was deeply moved. It was aethereal singing – not theatrical but beautifully controlled. When I came out into the blue starred sky, bells were ringing all over, and the cloisters were lit into angles with hurrying people.

DIARIES OF A YOUNG MYSTIC

I had spent the day watching the deer. How I love them, moving quietly. I love being without, pressed against the railing, unable to destroy the illusion of timelessness, the utter and absolute tranquillity. I came again to see them at lunch-hour on this sunny day, clutching a pork-pie down Holywell, alongside the turreted wall.

I still miss the warmth of people, but am hopeful now. The beauties of the world obsess me. I look everywhere with a hundred eyes, and the merest leaf is a kingdom. The buildings are tabernacles of filigree stone, and the students are moulded archetypes of studentship: youth, absorption and intellect. Children and cats I could gather into my heart – they seem so full of love.

And there is the music

Of the bells

Of the wind in the park trees

Of the clack of deer-horns

Of the words of poets.

There is the clear light of understanding and other people's explorations into Life and Meaning (eg. Tertium Organum, Eiseley, Einstein—currently reading.) How marvellous is intellect combined with emotion and questing! I am not the only one to see the wonderful world, but others also have preceded my own explorations. Within me, no tearing passions; only peace, contentment. For how long, O Lord?

Not desirable to last, I'll be bound. Anyway, even besides placidity and pride, I should become bored!

From my little universe to the world: War in the Middle East. It is a scene of horror. As I listen to news broadcasts, I am afraid of what I may hear. Kathy's (*my sister*) departure for Israel is postponed.

Monday 22nd October 1973

Life busies! Last week was a feast of music. Twice I was moved to tears, utterly transported by the most beautiful music-making I have ever heard. One occasion was hearing the New College choir sing 'When David Heard' by Tomkins, and the words "Absalom, my son...", ending with :..."would God I had died for thee". The final chord was constructed on eternity, maintained clear as a bell, while within the almost inaudible sound, faint echoes of melody were moving. So aethereal and pure, as if it would still be sounding when the last washes of humanity are no more.

Lyrical, eh!

And then on Saturday I sat among the candles in Magdalen Chapel and discovered a Britten I haven't known before with a setting of Eliot's 'Journey of the Magi' sung by three voices. Then 'Ovid's Metamorphoses' from a bodiless oboe streamed into the darkness.

And finally, 'Abraham and Isaac' This last I cannot describe: God's final "A-bra-ha-m" by both choir and counter-tenor after a finally wrought climax....well, I left earth behind! Wept for sheer beauty.

As I walked home through the Autumn leaves, I thought that now I no longer care whether I reach 'heaven' or not – I have had my share. Any more would be too great to bear – I'll settle for Purgatory!

"Music, when sweet voices die

Vibrates in the memory"

My own music-making has received a fillip: I sang with Brasenose Choir and twice to my incredulous ears heard people say of me: "Good alto" "Could hear you from the other side." Hope it spurs my confidence, though I'm secretly sure it's a case of successful bluff. I always *look* as if I'm singing gloriously! (Mouth widely enunciating, beatific expression etc.). I think I'll be very happy with this group, most civilised and enjoyable people!

Tuesday 30th October 1973

Happy Birthday, dear Lucy!

I have to wish it to myself, there being no one else around, as I prepare for another ordinary day. I face it with trepidation because yesterday was one of those days which was an unmitigated horror from beginning to end - nothing grave, just the smaller frustrations of life with which I cannot cope!

But today, being my birthday, here's hoping!

Saturday 3rd November 1973

It's been a ghastly week. Everything I have touched has gone wrong – every simple thing has complications! Which Great Thumbs Up has turned down?

"Knowledge and Love are one, and the measure is suffering."

LUCY OLIVER

Not long before I had moved from my first bed-sit in the Iffley Road to share a flat with a group of nurses living a little further up the same road. We were flat-mates, but not particularly friends, as we kept different time-scales, but it was a pleasant basement room.

Sunday 18th November 1973

It seems the dead of night, but it's only 5.30pm and has been dark for some time.

Winter Sundays alone in England will take some reckoning with. I have long found Sunday either a day of exquisite calm and joy, or a day of great sadness and loneliness. The more I do it, the less capable of living alone I find myself to be.

This room, white and be-pictured, is bland and empty. Last night I left in the middle of a concert because the chapel was so cold, the music cold (Byrd etc—very English; very incorporeal) and within I felt so cold that I could not withstand the aforementioned coldnesses. There was something polar-ish writhing around my heart and entrails.

I have been busy. Singing. Reading Milton's 'Samson Agonistes'. Concerts and things. O *(friend from Australia)* stayed last weekend. C and M came up the weekend before.

But it's cold this place!

Marvellous, rich, beautiful—but cold.

Wednesday 21st November 1973

Just finished PJ Kavanagh's *Perfect Stranger*, and was struck again by the beautiful quality of life as it can be, but so often, for so many, is not. He seems like a poetic spectator, a finely receptive instrument tuned into the currents of life. It stirred such longing in me to read of that great love, to know that it can exist. Is being 'unexpected' the key to its arising? If so, I have lost the game: it is the ongoing hope that suffuses my days.

She died, and he continued to live. This mystery is too great for comprehension or articulation. Perhaps in some dim way I do understand. It just was. She died. Not in payment of a debt for too much happiness; not as punishment; not even because her function in life was over; not as the richest gift she could give to him; not any of these, but simply the *fact* of her death.

Facts, '*what is*': these Ariel-like creatures in our experience are mere arrestations; silvery scales on the back of Time. All the world, all life, states and beings are composed of *facts*. We add the interpretation, wisely or otherwise.

Oh God, that I had more than eyes to appreciate all that is beautiful!! That I could weave these fragments into a more whole beauty and so help realize the Infinite!

I like his chapter on Oxford. I must be wary of this place; I recognize the dangers it holds and can feel their potency within me: the effortless way of playing with the heart-strings like a harp, inspiring bondage and servility; the ruinous somnolence of beauty; the web that can bind an eternal victim. Transience is necessary. I must draw from Oxford, but pass on.

I'm grateful that I have been able to move beyond the physical accidents of birth and circumstance, though Melbourne and Australia have given me so much. The privilege of making Oxford my own, and Cambridge, and all the world! After all this, if I cannot produce one pearl, I will have failed: committed the sin of turning from Truth for some selfish ends of my own no doubt.

I feel bent at the knees right now; such a trembling deep down. Because I will forget; every day, every hour I *forget*, and live as if there is nothing better to do but exist and fill in time. I grumble, despair, am restless, and what I Know, I forget!

How can this be? Why do I live behind a curtain? Is Truth too bright a glow to sustain? Would we burn out if we lived always in the consciousness of the true nature of things?

Help me to understand! I don't even understand why I don't understand!

Yesterday I sat in the Meadow in the low warm sun, and it seemed a dream that if I woke, I would cry to dream again. A familiar scene, yet every time different.

Friday 23rd November 1973

I have discovered that the way to make this room bearable is to live in it, to imbue it with thoughts and happy hours! No wonder it has been impersonal; I have never been here!

Lunched in Exeter today with JB (shy and sweet), and a couple of days ago in Christchurch with M (vivacious and bright young man padding across the frosty quad in carpet-slippers; chanting "Heloise" through the grill of the chapel quad, and aware of his own exuberance.) In moments of confidence, I want to direct Macbeth in the blackened chapel quad of Christchurch. In moments of sanity, I marvel at my impudence. But the idea remains with me.

Places are becoming charged with significance, which is the gift of being settled. Hours spent in the meadows; Tom Quad by full moon and the music of the choir, enhanced by a tall beautiful young man with golden hair, a voice worthy of Dante and hands fluid with some ageless grace and youthfulness; and who is also very aware of these qualities, and of my rapt perception of them!

Ah Lucy, ever the aesthete! What use your paeans of 'soul' when your senses are bemused by appearances?

Sunday 25th November 1973

A brilliant glimpse of stained glass through a forest of shadowy arches; a grill of intricately wrought iron; the shining wood of an angel carved on a pew, and wafting and weaving through them all, Vaughan Williams Mass in G minor in its true rite. What joy!

I had to clutch the pew, lest I end up somewhere among the roof bosses.

Monday 26th November 1973

Well, Kathy (*my sister*) came and went! What a genius for disorganization! I caught a taxi to Oxford station, we grabbed a sausage-roll, she had time to tell me there was a tiger in the case, and the train pulled out.

A fair young man was farewelling his girl. I will remember his face as the train left, that blank look of loss, his eyes watching down the track, dry-eyed pain. We humans are so easily wounded and flailed in our quivering tender centres!

So I am left with Kathy's precious objects in my keeping during her absence. (*The 'tiger' turned out to be stuffed!*) My first move was to play Alan Stivell *(Breton folk music)* and felt the memories flooding back of that vivid haunting night in Mikael's tiny cottage in Brittany in the snow. Also, of London of those early days after my arrival from Australia, when I was rootless, filling in time. All seem memories of another life, far from this here.

Travelling in Brittany the year before with a friend, I had encountered falling snow for the first time in my life, and was enchanted. We met a dark and beautiful young man named Mikael who invited us back to his isolated little cottage surrounded by white snowy fields, and played Breton music to us. It was so magical that it invoked a powerful experience a couple of years hence, when as part of my Kabbalist studies investigating the archangel Michael, I recalled Breton Mikael and invoked knowledge of the archangel. The sudden roar of energy and power in my ears terrified me and I quickly shut it down. I never tried investigating archangels this way again!

Thursday 6th December 1973

Oh, that figure with the golden hair! *(The chorister)* I want to meet and drink of that beautifulness, hedonist and sensualist that I am! I suspect it would go no further than the face, the voice, the fluid hands, the body – but give me that disillusionment! Until I am disillusioned, I sit on a knife-edge of wanting-ness, like a jackdaw entranced by a bright bauble! Entranced, not inspired; just entranced.

Sunday 9th December 1973

It's one of these nice timeless evenings by my solitary hearth. I leave my clock ticking soundlessly in my handbag, so the evening has no dimensions but those measured by my red-rimmed eyes.

One of the things I love about TS Eliot is the way that in the midst of a solid grey flow of words and ideas, the images are so brilliant and clear, standing out like rich carvings on shadowy architecture. My own poetry seems all of a same fleeting, flickering insubstantial quality, probably because of a preoccupation with the play of light and shadow, leaves in light etc. My whole opus (such as it is!) seems sort of spineless; nothing toothy!

I've been feeling rather a solitary eccentric lately. My independence is wearing thin!

There are poems in my head clamouring to be written. I don't understand the compulsion to crystallize and freeze all the colour and perfection of experiences, except that they are too marvellous to wash about in the recesses of memory alone. It's as if bringing them side by side and interacting, as perhaps they did not in actuality, gives birth to some new Whole. So much of the Present seems mere embryo. In recollection, substances can grow into fullness, no longer confined to temporality.

Monday 17th December 1973

I have been back to Cambridge for a long weekend. I sat on a bridge by Scudamore boat-yard, watching the ducks and waters race in the sunshine, and wallowed in King's chapel. There were no sad memories. I felt at home and at peace, with my memories swirling and being absorbed by the permanence and sameness of the place. Cambridge itself did not miss S, nor the summer gone. It is complete.

In King's College Chapel magnificent trumpeting angels stand black and free against the fluttering, filigree vault, one shining knee forward amid the caved folds of their garments, the silver trumpets almost audible. I see them as an image of the triumph of Man and Art, and I hope that the memory of their constant silent watch will comfort me in all the most abject moments to come.

The window facing the Backs, almost too perfect, rich and singing with gold in the afternoon sun. The altar makes no attempt to compete with the other glories; just that huge swirling Rubens, so quiet, loving, tender and fluid, emanating its own unique light. Not one jarring note, folly or misplaced line in the inter-play of forces in that Divine place. Yet it is deeply human, not awesomely full of transcendent strivings for some unreachable goal. Contained and unified, making of the Divine something one can understand and realize in a concrete way.

Sunday 31st December 1973

Well – the end of this year. Rather a bleak old end.

Hope for brighter things in the near-future.

The far-future, as fascinating as ever.

Sunday 6th January 1974

The new year is well advanced. I have been suffering from massive lethargy.

Today was different though; one Belgian, one Swiss, one Dane and me in a car. A proper activity for a bright Sunday! I felt immensely cheerful to be setting off on an excursion into Wales, and all the doldrums accumulated alone in my room vanished.

The Gloucester Cathedral cloister was surpassingly lovely and well-preserved. Under the intricate fan vaulting there were wraith-like monks, dappled by the window glass, and as quiet as the centuries since their passing. I wanted to fold my hands in imitation though they could neither see nor hear me through the wall of time.

Tintern Abbey was our final destination, just before sunset, in that grey valley. My imagination paved the brilliant grass with streaks of sun as I know it must so often be, and it felt like a place I have known all my life. I might have been the same shape myself, so perfectly did I fit.

CHAPTER 3
A Collection of Images

———

Sunday 13th January 1974

Gorged on cream crackers and fled indoors from a purple squall of rain and hail, I can't see through the streaming windows to the wet Iffley Rd.

What am I doing here? The question is posing itself frequently now, yet not really expecting an answer.

On that narrow hard bed and pillow, trying to arrange my shoulder so it is not squashed into numbness; punching the pillow under an aching and untired head; very desolate and full of memories – what am I doing here? So often lonely as I have never known it before – a physical isolation. Passing people in the street, thinking 'those are people I would like to know: lively, intelligent, interesting-looking people.' I'm feeling immensely sorry for myself! But still not letting the dam break on depression and despair. Funny: I still feel it is right to be here. No compulsion to move on or change my state.

But today as I walked by Merton wall, the whole cherished masonry and all it stands for seemed somehow effete, forced, almost degenerate. Only (*Thomas*) Hardy's line seemed apt:

"And the rotten rose is ript from the wall."

I've been engrossed in Fowles *The French Lieutenant's Woman*. An unexpectedly good novel: "a swarm of mysteries indeed" have tickled my mind. I'm fascinated by Duty, which I have never really understood, as I have always lived the precise opposite of Matthew Arnold's dictum to act only from duty or reasonableness, not from inclination. The Victorian age is a mystery to me, so much a product of my age as I am. I think I understand a little better now. Then, duty presupposed a whole structure, now quite demolished, so that one cannot even say that in a given situation, duty (as opposed to inclination) will be obvious, because it is not so. Duty to spare one person pain; duty to spare another; duty to oneself; duty to an ideal – thousands of duties clamouring to be followed.

What to do? Inclination seems the safest way out of the forest!

I am tired of self-sufficiency. I am weary of controlling my life, but am too wide-awake ever to cast myself on the tide, to drift at the mercy of the life all around, as so many do. At every step, I have chosen.

How many more years of this? 50? Perhaps less than one! I shouldn't moan, but if the latter is the case, get mighty busy!

My mind has become so boring lately. Obviously.

Sunday 27th January 1974

Gently hungover, but feeling alive and glad to be here in the sun at my window. Even daffodils on the sill.

Friday was my Inaugural dinner-party. So much preparation and planning but I enjoyed every minute of it. Generally successful. M & T were as I expected the chief sources of 'life'. Not the communal romp I would have liked. Dinner was not too disastrous, though nine people represented slightly larger capacities than I anticipated—the soup almost didn't make it!

M stayed to wash up and stayed overnight. I feel a slight conflict, but maintain moderation and discretion and an inner dedication to something not yet found. Reservation to guard the spiritual centres and the Holy Grail of love.

Last night was a party at T's. Crowded, thronging music and drink—just what I needed. Whole people, freed by alcohol and darkness from conventional utterance. T so familiar, a man of passage, incisive and developed of mind. Sitting in his room when most of the party had left, with another anthropologist, I felt suddenly stupid and female only. A male coterie of mind and knowledge from which I was excluded, not only by ignorance of Levi-Strauss and Frege, but by a different type of intellect, an operationally different mind.

This annoys me.

That there is a world in which I must be always outside, always one step behind following the thesis with effort. Not clever enough, I guess. But also, I feel that my mental leaps, my grasp is deeply rooted to more concrete (or more intangible) things than Mind, Holy Mind, Father Mind.

Have I no solid flesh at all?

Why do I feel evanescent, composed of air, fire and water; a sort of porcelain vessel to be filled, and constantly breakable? I feel hollow.

Is a woman most complete in the act of love when all that male mind is concentrated totally on her, on her body and engaged on a level of not-thought? Where she is secure and in command? I know I insult women of intellect much greater than mine.

I need to intervene here to comment on these first rumblings of discontent about a certain type of academic intellectualism of which, at this stage of not yet taking up higher studies at the university, I was in awe. Later I joined the club and learned to speak the language, Levi-Strauss and all. Having mastered it, I was then bored by the intellectual game, and reverted to the evanescent and intangible which is far more interesting!

With longer acquaintance, as T and I were an item for more than a year, I also found this rational-mind-framing much less impressive, and remember noticing with an inner yawn later on, that if I exerted myself, I could 'run rings around' him in argument. That realization became something of an awakening, and I became more secure in a different type or quality of intellectual activity, recognizing that both types are possible. Neither was I wrong to recognize how men typically enjoy the display of mental prowess, which on this occasion, I had found so alienating.

Thursday 31st January 1974

Two nights of our performance of *Dyskalos* with the Drama club over! There were some fabulous shambles.

Last night, four pages of the play were omitted in a dramatic leap from Act IV to Act V without anyone noticing, and sans interlude!

Both nights featured prolonged moanings by a character who couldn't remember his lines. He ran around holding his head and adlibbing groans, whilst repeating the few lines he did know, and ignoring helpful cues from his fellow-actors trying to help him escape from the stage!

Then tonight, after fluttering around like an autumn leaf, as we three women recited our 'cicada' poem cross-legged on the floor, when we stood up to leave, I discovered my foot was hopelessly entangled in the voluminous hem of my skirt. Therefore, instead of floating gracefully off the stage after the others, I began to hop up and down like a peachy whip in my efforts to free it. The lights burst on. Then tactfully went off, as I was still hopping on one leg with my bottom to the audience, and wondering how on earth I was going to get off the stage.

Long minutes and many audience titters later, I managed to free my leg and I shot off through the back of the stage.

Ah! The joys of being a thespian! It is a joy however. I have few stakes in this production, so the more things go wrong the more I enjoy it!

Aye, and work is so boring. Books and darkness drag out the hours (*it was the year of national unrest and strikes, with prolonged power cuts, so the bookshop was often operating dimly with the help of candles. Less romantic than being a great nuisance!*) I live for people calling in to see me. At one point today, feeling 'got at' by N in his tactless way, everything swam out of proportion, and life at Parkers loomed important, intricate and tinged with misdeed and failure. Miserably, I fought to re-establish some balance in my view of life, but it's hard to find anything to cling to. My life is suddenly busy, but something is wrong. Somewhere there are values missing. Everything I touch seems sordid because I have no governing ideal at present.

Until now there was always my Grand Love, the shining knightly ideal, and many other ideals of going, seeing, doing, being. But now I've come, seen, done and been, and the Great Love has crumbled to dust; one of life's blind alleys. Unrealizable.

I'm treading a delicate path with M. I enjoy him, but don't want to lead the poor lad into involvement. I see how he sees me, but it's not Me, and it's an ignoble face he sees. I also know what attracts me to T, and it is equally as ignoble. All good company and friends though; I shouldn't get all intense and worried about either situation. I guess I want to 'fall in Love' with the highest shining part of me. Everything else is tin, tarnished, even friendships seem hollow. I miss close women friends, for these do not get complicated with sexual currents.

Monday 4th February 1974

Lucy, my girl, this cannot go on. I am behaving in a most irresponsible fashion.

Merely to humour a careless whim of mine, M procured strawberries from Fortnum and Mason to eat with champagne! Dear boy, I must not accept such gestures, playing at Zuleika Dobson and disturbed at heart. Turn over a new leaf or perish.

Thursday 14th February 1974

Fascinating things surrounding me at present. I'm more 'engaged' than I've ever been before, I think; I never have a night at home. It's watching people flux and change, and relationships altering, expanding and shrinking by turns!

This morning I was very much out of joint with the world and feeling worm-like. Then I went walking at lunchtime to see the deer and the great lake which now is Magdalen Meadow. Whereupon I dared to stand up again, as just the little fascinations of the physical natural world healed and soothed what was uneasy.

Thursday 21 February 1974

Walking back from dinner in Hall at Magdalen, hearing the clack of my heels in the quiet street on a mild night.

Dinner involved silver candlesticks and cutlery, white cloth and all the ritual I like so much. At one end of the table sat a Spanish count with an enormous floppy bow around his cultured neck. Another pretentious—ah, no, I mean 'colourful'—person offered snuff from a small silver snuff box. I drew on my cigar and surveyed the Oscar Wilde Rooms, and drew up plans with P for summer parties on the river and all that summer myth which is the Oxford idyll. Seems attractive, I must say!

To dally in this small centre of the universe, where printed names become actual people and relations of people, rendering the whole scale and strata of 'social hierarchy' a hollow, flimsy gown, dissolving into just People! And people in two classes: boring and interesting. In degrees of course, and all strictly relative—to me!

P emerges and emerges. Someone I may become very fond of—distinctly humorous, warm and appreciative.

This evening is stored as one of the Collection of Images of my life here.

I see other images, such as ploughman's lunches and mead at the Turf, surrounded by tipsy roofs and pigeons with an unaccountable M, by turns undergraduate, poet, sage, Jew, Englishman, woman-distruster, woman-worshipper, boy, man.

I see a long path winding between shining sheets of water: Magdalen Walks in flood, just as I saw in my dreams several weeks ago. White milky water at evening, and rootless trees rising in the waters. Surreal great roots of an elm sent crashing in the gales which rocked Oxford. Yet all untouched, the bluebells and crocuses are tentatively opening for Spring.

I hear a bird, a night bird calling before the dawn, where all night long water dripped and dripped from the eaves of an open window. I see a figure, myself, wrapped like a refugee in blanket, kneeling before the window and breathing in great draughts of the night air. Still that dripping water in the black ivy and eaves. The room beyond, all warm and tousled....

Friday 22nd February 1974

Heard again 'Abraham and Isaac'. If last time I heard it with tears of joy, tonight was too close to pain to be joy. It lays me out utterly!

These two struggling for faith, and finding it together in the Godhead—this triangle of faith and great crisis, resolved with a decision to trust the command of some vasty Providence.

Isaac spreadeagled as Christ: "Do with me what you will". I saw it as an image of crucifixion transfixed across the history of the world, with arms like a Grunewald, hands supplicating, and hung like the Dali on a little globe.

There is really no choice for us to escape this iconography; we are forced historically to live under its shadow. And it is so fine, so beautiful; the grandest of gestures made concrete. Truth acted out on an enormous stage, once and for all. As a Word made flesh, Truth is made Act, made Fact.

How I wish I could detach the Christ, His words and the whole schema from the cloying interpretations and images forcibly fed into my psyche when young. Hard to see beyond them, hard to move; horrible images, life-defying, twisted into shapes. Not the images of poetry, but of dogma and death. By images, I mean not the actual content, nor the intention (of the best) but the shadowy world of spirit and the life of Symbols which can so easily be rendered impotent and prescribed, so they are no longer the stuff of poetry.

However, all is fine right now, when I can sit with a glass of sherry listening to the Lamentation of Jeremiah, and watching smoke curl up into the darkness gathering at the windows.

Winter is leaving.

Sunday 24th February 1974

Oh, gorgeous morning!

Down by the river and barges, two swans are turning and moving with perfect synchronization as in a ballet, each leaving a wake of light and dazzling water.

The Meadows and the morning are being thoroughly appreciated by hordes of diverse people, dogs and children. Tiny figures with blue hoods and bandy legs are hiding behind trees and daffodils, climbing logs, and running open-legged under the elms. So, so fascinating; so absolutely expressive and immediate.

Here shall I sit in the sun, all day if need be, till the joy of Sunday morning is spent.

Earlier I woke in Christchurch to sun and bells, streams of bells; belling the hours and quarter-hours; urgent bells signalling; carillons of bells ringing the morning in Oxford.

I looked over the roofs, spires, slates, pinnacles, tree branches and basking stone of the heart of the city. Felt all the joy of the morning, but also that it is evanescent; it has no roots, and this is almost sadness.

Yesterday I played tennis with M. However, in addition to the ball, the surrounding brilliant fields, the warm sun tossing its light from big westerly clouds and the river of a Saturday afternoon all competed for my attention. Unfortunately for M, my leisurely strokes and the soft pat of the strings were more symbolic than in earnest! It was like being part of some fantastic ballet of youth and liberation.

I am a romantic twit, but it is these memories I want to keep, when being human and alive is positively a pleasure. The whole 'Oxford

Thing' has always loomed large in my imagination—being young in Oxford seems one of the finest and most privileged experiences. Perhaps one day I may also know Love, stability and children, and then there could be no more to ask of one life.

An undergraduate party last night in Balliol, with plenty of drink, gaiety, hoarse singing, tickling, watching a few tottering lads savouring the beginnings of independence and a naïve attempt at debauchery.

Later: I went to see Manitas di Plata again! Bella! Such consummate art. Hearing the rhythms of the blood: passion, lyricism, violence. I went with D, who was also hopping about in her seat with enjoyment, as she is so vital and continental. At one point, Manitas held his guitar and made bell-like sounds: "Les cloches de La Camargue", he said. What an image! I see Proust's golden flèches moving across a vast plain.....

Wednesday 27th February 1974

Down by the river this afternoon watching Torpids boat-race, it was a freezing day, which is most unusual. With frozen nose and numb lips in the rugged cold of real winter, we watched the first race rowed in snow! Met M, numb and be-hatted. We drifted across the river in a punt to the haven of the boathouses. There we took tea with battenburg cake, watching the Eights stroking cleanly upstream, and cheering P as the Magdalen 2nd Division sweated rhythmically past.

I liked the slim energetic bodies of the rowers, and the hoarse partisan shouts of the supporters. But perhaps I'm getting old, as I was spectator rather than participant. Sometimes I feel a little uneasy with M, as if out of my proper element. His world no longer completely fits me I suppose, like a suit which has grown too small and is baggy at the knees and elbows. M himself is interesting—where he is independent of the world around, (ie. where everyone is most interesting!) when slipping in and out of many facets, non-categorizable (who was it said that of me? and resonant with many different sounds.

By contrast, some people give off a dull boom-boom, like double-basses, or worse, like the persistent thump of amplified pop music. P is another interesting fish in the aquarium. He works in quite a different way from above mentioned sheening fish; more like a crab or anemone opening out gradually, feeling with the play and tug of the waters.

Better stop with this before I have all my friends swimming about in aquatic form!

Stella Maris.

Sunday 3rd March 1974

It's a worming thought, that I am not capable of a great Quest! If I have neither the intellect, courage nor tenacity for a great achievement, what is left? Just days and more days, pleasures and discontents. Perhaps if I can admit that I am not capable of taking the world on my shoulders, there will be an end to fretting, to the gnawing sensation that there should be something more, that I should be doing Something but am not.

"Oh weariness of heart! I would be free

to seek my God in some eternity,

where no road ever came, no foot draw nigh,

and no man ever yet

brought gifts, or burned the sweet

incense of rapt, forlorn austerity" *(J Redwood Anderson)*

" I, even I, am he who knoweth the roads

through the sky and the wind thereof is my body." *(Ezra Pound)*

Ah, Lucy, tu es petite! My road is my own, but it is not likely to cut a swathe. And why should it? There is need for people of direction, not for vainglory.

What gives shape to the day by day? How do we steer the minute, and give purpose to the hour?

Tuesday 5th March 1974

Nothing heightens perception of decadence so much as an encounter with its opposite. What is goodness? Is goodness wholesomeness—like a loaf of farm bread? Dull and bland? No. And yet, yes.

I cannot reconcile these two streaks in me:

— one which hungers for colour edged with black, for sharpness and brilliance of surface, and the other, a thirst for innocence, sparkling whiteness and total wide-eyed embracing of all that is beautiful and Good.

Both are present and alternate in different contexts. As per William Blake of course. They co-exist within the same being, and each regards an unrelieved expanse of the other as absolute Dullness and Boredom! Evil is ultimately unsatisfying and disturbing. Goodness tends to naïve optimism and can be nauseous as wedding-cake in large quantities. Also lacks tension and is passive and non-creative.

I am left with the rather trite conclusion that a true perception of goodness can only come from an acquaintance with badness. As in William Blake: from Innocence to Experience and back to Innocence again, but this time a transcendent Innocence, an aware and vital Innocence built on experience, and *chosen*.

Where are all the wise men? The Educators? They rise up periodically and transcend their historical setting, eg. Christ, Buddha; or great artists: Dante, Michelangelo et al, but then are seized upon and distorted. The message is still there, but each of us must discover it anew, increasingly difficult to do with centuries of overlay. We need more of these Educators, these Shining Ones. There is a desperate need for a re-statement of the message of Christianity. A new Messiah, or many Messiahs, for perhaps from now we cannot expect the varieties of humankind to conform to any one pattern.

How long, Oh Lord? How long?

But I will still rejoice in brilliance, darkness, black, white, crimson and burning yellow, for these are the stuff of life. I eschew all pastels—these feeble compromises, except where they have the lucent substance born of Light.

How can I ever know what I am? I am everything and nothing.

Why should I seek to know? To have power over the forces of life in me, and hence others?

No, not good enough! I must learn to understand these forces, not just seek to control them.

Where is wisdom?

To be wise as the blossom, wise as the daffodil and blood-rose, wise as the lily in the valleys and the bloated peony-flower......seek this.

Wednesday 6th March 1974

Another enjoyable dinner at Nuffield last night, and tonight I dined at Trinity High Table with F, a lengthy ritual presided over from our High Island table above a sea of black gowns and babbling faces in a dignified panelled room. The mahogany table was laid with fruit and port. This was a new experience. I chatted with the President of the college, a gracious, sensitive broad man, the sort who restores one's faith in Academics. Our final watering-place was the common room for coffee.

From there we accompanied a bright Ceylonese Law tutor to the Old Trinity Library. It was a ghost-spotting expedition, instigated by a conversation about the ghost of Cardinal Newman who lived, and has since *been seen* near Rv's rooms!! (Apparently!)

The 13th century library was lovely. Brown, dusty and filled with calm, and above all, history. Very rarely can I muster any communication with the past, but I could not avoid it as I held the book donated by Henry VIII, and ran my finger over the signature of his Lord High Chancellor of England, dated 1560 or thereabouts. There was an 18th century guide book to the

Univerſitieſ of Oxford and Cambridge, phrased with the utmost delicacy and charming poetic prose, and very sensitive to the weather and airs of Oxford. Such and such a place may have "breeſeſ from the North, but is bathed in sunshine in Summer..."etc.

In a large old chest are mouldering a pile of letters, mostly in official vein, but crackling with age and faded ink and many bearing heavy red and black seals, broken open in the seventeenth century. I was totally fascinated, rummaging (gently) through these voices from people so long silent. They became almost real; their human writing and ordinary sentiments more real than preserved high Art which has a different sort of immediacy.

No actual ghosts appeared, unfortunately. Not even Cardinal Newman introduced himself in the dark panelled room which is Rv's study, nor even the gentleman who suicided by drinking poison there.

Sunday 10th March 1974

The ecstasy of one's own fireside! I feel like a cat curled up in a rug with a red glow of heat on my face while reading of the cold, wet exhaustions of walking from Land's End to John O'Groats in my current book. The swish of cars in the sludge of the Iffley Road.

And sludge it is. Woke this morning to snow, thick on the rooftops and meadows. Hooded figures picked their way through the flakes, an occasional cleric, or strange apparitions with caps, black cloaks and tall implements of ritual: for it is Sunday in Oxford! I soon joined them, sliding and slipping through the ice while holding my long skirt out of the worst icy pits. The Merton daffodils poked valiantly through the blanket. Birds hopped and pecked at clumps of grass. At Magdalen, the deer looked dignified and completely at home in their whitened park.

Unfortunately, walking was too difficult to permit lengthy rambles. I fell over once, without dismay, though my crepe skirt shrank into itself in a most peculiar way, reminiscent of the time I was caught in a rainstorm going to work, and arrived at Parkers with my long skirt shrivelled to about mid-calf. It took all morning for it to dry, and I gave interested persons bulletins about its progress as it gradually grew longer and longer to reach my shoes again.

Sunday mornings are fabulous, but Sunday afternoons should not be spent alone. I always hunger for companionship—anyone's.

Friday night T gave a dinner party for his tutor and wife. T is an excellent cook: I ate so much I thought I could never eat again. Then the party made a sally round to the anthropologist N's flat, where a cool crew of African musicians were grooving at their own groovy music-making. The small room vibrated to the thunderous sounds from an open grand piano and the tom-toms of beer-cans. While these painted birds of paradise—I felt them to be slightly ludicrous in a contrived western aping of their more primitive (ie. more sophisticated) countrymen—created bedlam, a calm African woman sat like carved wood in a corner. Around her and like her, was the silence of the beautiful collection of native objects d'art the anthropologist has gathered. Eclectic, exotic, guarding anthropological mysteries I could only dimly sense.

I took a particular fancy to a little flat wooden frog with one and a half breasts, feeling the assurance of holding the cool smooth wood. Would love to know its origin. And one of the most exquisite objects I have ever seen was the Japanese screen by the door. Dark and shining, it blossomed into a fall of jacaranda flowers, birds, twigs: all carved in ivory or mother-of-pearl. Tiny leaves were scattered like snow.

Proportionately as the noise level rose, I felt a silence and stillness amounting to stasis welling within. Perhaps I was mesmerised by it all, or perhaps it was a reaction to the discords present in that gathering, not least of which was the 'cult' surrounding this anthropologist. The brighter-than-bright surface of Mind and intelligence aware of its own worth. For me, it was brittle artifice in a carnival-world, playing to the ring, gaudy, gay, and aimed at keeping at bay the encroaching night outside. There is a tragic face to eccentricity or image-creation. True, all of us must have a mask, but some are more brittle than others.

Tuesday 12th March 1974

An evening to plan our Ireland expedition. We four, T & P and B, P's visiting girl-friend, spread out our maps and guides over dinner at The Trout, where suitably, the waters 'raced' in the darkness beside us. Then we adjourned to The Perch for further perusal and drank green chartreuse, and finally adjourned to the Magdalen MCR where we were greatly entertained by Magdalen's own professional magician. Wonderful to see handkerchiefs appearing from people's ears, objects disappearing and re-appearing in a delightful confusion of reality.

I'm looking forward to Ireland. I hope we manage to stand each other for a week.

LUCY OLIVER

Thursday 14th March 1974

Yesterday T and I went for a drive into the countryside, setting off after lunch on a cloudy/sunny day. Called at Stonesfield to see R whom I liked very much during Dyskalos. We made for Great Tew, and I actually drove the car and enjoyed being behind the wheel after so long. I negotiated a few rather interesting corners, avoiding oncoming lorries and careless pedestrians without gears, since I couldn't concentrate on everything at once. But on the whole I didn't do anything too silly considering my inexperience.

Great Tew was the archetypal English village. The sun was low and golden on the common and the windows of the cottages when we arrived. All were thatched, many becoming derelict, the thatch now chewed and dark like the ivy-invaded windows. In the shadow of a hill a small row of cottages lay under trees and brambles. Children, released from their small school-house, stalked from oak to oak and in and out the cottages.

Then we drove out of the village to the church, and walked down a long green pathway with daffodils and white clumps of snow still scattered there in the late afternoon sun, and a forest of grey headstones. T snapped busily, and I rued my lack of film to capture the calmness.

We drove on, and stopped to watch a crimson sun form itself in the sky. Torn out of a blank grey sky, it hung there at the end of the road between the bare hedgerows. In a quest for a sympathetic pub, we ended at The Perch in Binsey, where we sat like two ancient sages before the fire for several hours, pussy cat on laps.

Such a nice day. I could drive like that forever. Work today was hideous. The place is becoming tension-ridden for me, with N flapping around like an old hen. Will leave soon.

T and I paddle along together. The endearing thing about him is that he knows what he is; knows his limitations and insecurities. He's generous, kind, warm and in need of affection, and very comfortable. If he is also clumsy and lacking in ease, he knows it. His self-consciousness, bluster and name-dropping tendencies are all symptoms of a very straight, even naïve boy within. Even this he seems to recognise. I think of him with affection, but I think my silences will grow.

Of whom do I think now, as Spring approaches and idealism flutters into new life? The "voice of the turtle" is heard again, the voice of something so noble and complete, that to dream is sadness. I think I must always keep a dream, for without it, everything is dross and meaningless. Down to the deeps, to the core of my real being which once was moved. It seems the only emotion capable of giving birth.

This is a reference to the great unrequited love which haunted my years at Melbourne University, the inspiration for many soulful musings and dreams chronicled in my earlier diaries, and which I finally laid to rest by following the thread across the world for a final chance to see if those dark eyes could ever look on me with recognition. The answer was no, and I left it behind.

Thursday 21st March 1974

Evening. The sun is settling behind the Iffley Road houses, across the playing-fields, the river, the Meadows, Tom Tower after a warm Spring-like day. The first dribbles of Spring are treacherous, I fear.

I hate leaving the town again now that the evenings are long. The world is very active about 6pm with workers heading home, students in caps and gowns discussing the afternoon's exam papers, birds very noisy, buses and cars streaming across Magdalen Bridge. Soon it will be warm enough to sit in the Meadows contemplating the evening hours.

"You're basically a quiet, thoughtful girl aren't you", said T once. I, of course, was slightly put out at this image; other people's limited summations of one's character never tally with the variety and scope of one's own vision of oneself! But I suppose I am, and must accept what I am and what I love. And I love to be meditative, to curl thoughts like cigarette smoke, or more often, just to sit like a sponge absorbing.

Magdalen Walks are bordered by daffodils and bluebells. I don't quite believe that these flowers are real, springing up so elegantly and suddenly, and so cunningly arranged. It's all too chocolate-boxy for one accustomed to less cultivated nature Down Under. I expect to have to pay for something as glorious as a daffodil, not get hundreds of them for free!

I gave another supper-party last night. Unfortunately, I was suffering from the previous day's food poisoning (lunch at the K.A) so didn't relish the food. In fact, when I tipped half a gallon of soup all over my jumper, skirt and floor, I wondered why the hell I got these crazy ideas of playing Lady Hostess.

CHAPTER 4
In the Backyard of the Poet

———

Saturday 23rd March 1974

First night out in Wales at a huge mock-Elizabethan mansion converted into a hostel. Big panelled windows and window-seats.

I stood outside in the grounds briefly before we set off for the town and food. It smelled of evening and England, that cool smoky peace of so many evenings I have stood outside strange hostels; of Rydal last year in the evening hours, of falling in love and waterfalls. How lovely!

Wenlock Edge for lunch in an old pub, and then to stand on the Edge and peer through the mist down the sheer side to a glimpse of fields. It was all Housman and Vaughan Williams. I tried to soak in the feel of Shropshire.

Strange empty morgue-like pub this evening. 'Tis a lovely England, this auld country, this literary land!

Tuesday 26th March 1974 Clonkeen – Co Kerry

End of second day in Ireland. Our Sunday in Wales was very pleasant, lunching on bread and cheese high on a windy road in Snowdonia. Such wild craggy country! Watched a farmer round up his sheep with the help of crook, sheep dogs and small boy.

The ferry journey passed bearably. Much waiting involved, so we were weary as we drove into Dublin on Monday morning. Our faux-Irish accents, which had started developing in Wales were in full swing. It is becoming too easy and a little wearisome, but quite irresistible! The voices are charming!

Dublin is full of fascination. A conglomerate city with a remarkably successful mixture of awful new building, preserved splendour and hideousness, with some lovely places like Bewley's Oriental café which was a revelation. It is true Ireland never moves on; it is a collection of 'periods' still vibrant in their original character. Bewleys is pure nineteenth century, with wooden panelling etc. Just the sort of place I have always wanted for the odd cup of coffee, but never realized! One of the (many) pubs we patronised was of the same style and vintage, just never altered or renovated. Frothy Guinness is likely to be our downfall!

Down South, Glendalough over the bleak Wicklow Hills brought us our first ruins and the typical round tower where the monks used to scuttle with their valuables. A whispering history indeed; even I can feel the past very strongly. The Wicklow Hills and Sally Gap were utterly desolate; hardly the call of a bird. Miles and miles of black peat as if some mighty fire had swept through and gutted the last vestiges of mankind. The most desolate place I have ever seen.

Today we have spent driving mostly, and lunched on the estuary of the river Tay. For the first time this holiday there was no mist or fog, but sunshine all day, so the water sparkled where we ate our lunch with sea-gulls on the rocks.

Most lovely, like the lake we found last night hidden in the hills, and calm as a mirror between the mountain sides. It was there we discovered that the boot of the car had jammed, which necessitated a trip to Laregh, and the employment of a family of dark haired, freckled Irish, who tumbled out of a large four-storey house set among pines. I seized the opportunity to go on a little walk alone to feel the evening.

Constant company is a bit wearying, and particularly this company. It was immediately apparent that we are no foursome. I'm almost used to it now, but I was disappointed at first. To be as kind as possible, B seems insecure, and lovely like a doll made of cardboard or tinsel. "A pain", as T put it bluntly. I'm coming to accept it now, but am still surprised that P should desire a creature who seems to fulfil the stereotype of a pretty bit of fluff, who has so far manifested little evidence of an ability to have an opinion let alone think or make less predictable remark! Strange are the ways of men! But I'm being bitchy! Perhaps I'm jealous—she is so perfect! (Though it would be nice if she could acknowledge our existence as members of the expedition!)

With hindsight, as a shy visitor, she was probably intimidated by the whole Oxford milieu. She found her feet eventually, and things went better!

P has emerged considerably, as a strong, decisive personality who can be most amusing. However, he's not at his best with B, and overall, I'm slightly disillusioned. With T too, I sometimes feel rather impatient (this is what travelling does!) just because his manner is so wearisome with its monotonous string of epithets! "Dear old T", I think when he's being calm and intelligent, but soon I'm irritated by constant contact. So, there be tensions, though underneath, not on top, and generally we're all happy and enjoying the trip.

We met a wonderful woman tonight who made us sandwiches and tea in the house where she was born, is raising her sweet-voiced children, and will probably die. I was fascinated by her warmth, her maturity, her lovely eyes. She married a boy from a few cottages down the road, so they have two cottages, from which they farm, plant potatoes and milk cattle.

And all around are the hills, the Paps near Killarney.

Friday 29th March 1974 Connemara

Evening on the lake, with small boats rocking and all the craggy mountains reflected in the still water. It is just superb. We walked along a little road from the hostel here, where the philosopher Wittgenstein had lived. Little stone cottages were open to the prying eye; wiry children stood on the walls and gaped at the well-dressed intruders; a baby lamb bleated and tottered across the grass. We are right on one of the most westerly tips of Ireland. It is so calm, so full of the calm of some other age, that it seems hardly real for so twentieth-century a person, full of haste and craving of stimuli.

And today, the apotheosis: Yeats Tower and Coole Park!

We stumbled across it unexpectedly, this ancient tower at Thoor Ballylee, so deeply resonant for me. Suddenly, as we drove along a small road, there appeared in front of us an ivy-covered tower, with crumbling battlements, crevices and jackdaws, and I recognised it.

Very quiet. The waters raced from under the bridge on a warm grey morning.

On the rocks at the back of it lay a dead sheep, its skin tight like parchment, its ribs decayed. 'Dead in the backyard of the poet', I thought. I felt he would have appreciated the scene, and drawn something from it.

Coole Park was strange. The house is gone. We found the tree with signatures and I made out a wobbly WBY, and AE in a triangle, and a sprawling GBS (George Bernard Shaw). Walking along the lake. I felt very close to the man who wrote of the wintry trees and mounting swans. Two swans I saw, winging through the trees, and it was all very bleak. The water was not brimming on the blackened reaches.

Sunday 31st March 1974

Our last Sunday in Ireland in the Glen of Acherlow. And broke. Due to a slight miscalculation, we have about 50p and the ferry fare!

P & B left us today to take the train to London. It was almost sad to break up our little party—we had learned to live with each other! We had come to accept B, who had come to accept T. All in all, we made quite a happy little group.

Last night we spent on the windswept rocky side of the inlet near Achill Island, and awoke to the blue, green, purple and white-studded landscape so typical of Ireland.

One of my happiest memories was the day we spent cycling on Valentia Island. How I enjoyed the freedom and feeling of mobility, the sense of merging with the landscape as we toiled up hills and sped down on our blue cycles, and the wonderful views.

One amusing incident occurred when we came upon a vast slope of slate and quarry. Lower down was an amazing grotto and waterfall housing a statue of the Virgin and St. Bernadette, and far beneath the cave proper, we could see fountains, altar, rails etc and two workmen, who were busy painting the rails blue and cream. We stood admiringly on the top of that high and sheer hill of slate, and I gave my bicycle to T to hold while I photographed him.

Typically, he let the bike fall over. Predictably, my camera shot from the basket and started off on a journey down the slate hillside. Also predictably, T set off after it in one stupendous bound, sliding down the slates on his bottom to reach the camera at the foot of the hill.

We onlookers stood stunned throughout the whole precipitous performance, initially too startled at the drama even to laugh!

I think of all the Guinness we have consumed, thick and frothy, in many a strange little bar peopled with black-suited, red-faced Irishmen. The Black Fantastic.

And all those donkeys on the roads—most amusing animals. We stopped one day for lunch in a landscape of blue and yellow by a rushing stream, and I wandered away and stood singing, thinking how strange it was to be here in Ireland, so familiar from imaginings and traveller's tales.

No other thoughts worth mentioning. It's time I fell in love again—I've forgotten how to think!

DIARIES OF A YOUNG MYSTIC

Wednesday 3rd April 1974

For T and me the last two days of our trip were very pleasant, with a leisurely drive through Ireland on Monday and the usual picnic lunch up a tiny lane on boggy green grass.

The ferry trip was bearable until we arrived in Fishguard at 1am. The hotel was full, and the motel iniquitously expensive, especially given our straightened circumstances, so we rebelled and drove our car to a hillside. There we spent the most uncomfortable night I can remember, huddled on the back-seat of the car which rocked and rattled in the wind and rain of a convenient storm. Cold and stiff, we saw the dawn come, and cranked ourselves into life to seek loo, petrol and breakfast in that order.

Wales is lovely. We called at Laugharne again, in sunshine this time. I did not feel inspired, but very at home there and knew it so well.

With me at the wheel, we detoured up a spectacular mountain and halted at the top to survey the plotted and pieced landscape. Unfortunately, we were forced to remain halted for several hours, as no doubt influenced by my delicate wrenches, the gears went soggy and refused to co-operate, and the knob came off in my hand to T's dismay and my chagrin. Eventually, we managed a lift to a small cottage down the mountainside, where a young yogic couple lent us their phone and beautiful living-room until the AA came to our rescue.

Uneventful but enjoyable drive past all the so-called 'perfect pubs' flaunted by the Welsh countryside. T and I, surprisingly, were getting on well these three days together. Too well; I am becoming a little uneasy and wondering whether he is becoming too fond of me, more so than I of him. It's all so easy and comfortable.

Tuesday April 9th 1974

Mired in a bog of decisions. I'm leaving Parkers in two days. Each day is so long – I have well outstayed my enthusiasm. Yet I will very much miss the company; such an extraordinarily friendly, amusing, relaxed lot of people. I shall be quite sad on Thursday, and I know they are sorry I'm leaving too. Ah well!

Kathy (*my sister*) has returned penniless and cured of travelling. Mary & Ken (*another sister and her husband*) are returning to Australia in just over a month. This will be a serious wrench. I'm dreading the feeling of aloneness which will inevitably ensue unless I'm feeling very happy and secure in some activity or way of life.

Last Sunday I spent six hours punting on the river in Spring sunshine with some friends. We moored by a meadow for lunch. Later we moored and wandered in the Magdalen Fellows Garden where there were banks of Spring flowers, Shakespearean in their profusion: violets, primroses, grape hyacinths, daffodils and daisies. So beautiful—it was a paradise transfixed through flowers.

Then our paddle disappeared from where it lay on the floral bank. In an astonishing mythic transformation, I found myself marching fiercely into a neighbouring park to recover it, following a righteous instinct which led me straight to the young felons. I demanded its return in an awe-inspiring manner, delivering my most telling blow with the words: "And what were you doing anyway in that private garden?" !!! They failed to call my bluff!

None of us were Magdalen Fellows! As we continued punting up the river, I wondered what had come over me: an uprising of calm laser-like intent, x-ray vision and absolute purpose. Me, but not-me.

Friday 20th April 1974

If I'm to retain any mental flexibility at all I must exercise my mind!

The film *The Exorcist* provoked heated debate between T & myself. I can accept that 'forces' can exist as abstract and complete entities, though unable to manifest without the medium of matter. The force between cause and action could be seen as an 'entity'. We can abstract it, and so talk about 'the force of love'. That is 'Love'.

Therefore, I think it is reasonable to postulate the existence of an extreme, an 'absolute' force, ie. God, or perhaps a Devil. If this force can collect like a raging lion, and seize randomly some person for its vehicle of expression, it is earthed like a lightning-bolt through a conductor.

What use is transcendent vision in the melee of life?

How can one push any particular line when twenty opposing views seem equally true in some measure? Surely shimmering truth requires a careful weighing, balancing, synthesizing and isolating of all the myriad forces of an issue, generalizations as well as particular manifestations of it, all the impinging factors etc.

But that means argument gets bogged down in a thousand entirely *relevant* side-tracks! To deliberately disregard any of them constitutes dishonesty or blindness!

Oh complexity!

LUCY OLIVER

Sunday 22 April 1974

I set off across the fields in the warm four o'clock afternoon. Smell of cows and grass. Found my little lane and sat on the edge of a vast rolling plain of what I decided to christen 'alfalfa', because I do not know what alfalfa is, and I don't know what this coarse grassy substance is either.

Into the warm breast of the sun, I read Wallace Stevens' 'Sunday Morning'.

"Death is the mother of beauty." Good to hear the words aloud against the wind in the grass, and swallowed up to be part of the landscape like the hum of an articulate bee.

Then I went knee-deep across the alfalfa field to a small green wood. Watched horses stepping like porcelain, and on a flower-dotted field I sat for a long time as the sun's intensity grew lower, and read 'Credences of Summer', which was a perfect selection and came to life as I've never understood it before. Here I was in perfect contentment and fullness surveying the English landscape of myth:

"...green's green apogee"

"...This is the barrenness

Of the fertile thing that can attain no more"

Stevens is always exploratory. I waited with bated breath for the resolution of the problem; this barrenness of completeness; this "arrested peace".

But no solution.

So, I decided that, yes, without desire, without the "physical pine, metaphysical pine" there is no movement. At fullness or apogee there is only rest and absorption. This may be vital experience, but also vital is the "averting", and the "singing about"; for without the ability to distance from it, experience cannot be fully recognised.

The flickering eye creates a total image, so experience must flick from absorption to distance. Art is produced by knowing what time is for what, like a violinist. But here the instrument is Being. Death is an essential part of the rhythm, because no moment ever lasts. Even my moment on the hillside has a pre-ordained end: the sun sinks, it becomes chilly, dark; I am stiff. It is over.

Similarly, the 'moment' of life comes to an end, and therein lies its beauty. Joy is the knowledge of transience.

Sunday 28th April 1974

Tonight, I am conscious of the void.

I see a trail of life behind me, a wake of light like Wynken, Blynken and Nod, and ahead—just winds. Reaching out, searching the eyes of passers-by, the flight to arms where the warm haze of another's presence dulls vision and fills the windy cracks of wanting-ness — Ai-ee! They pass! It all passes.

Which is true life: the busy coating of peripheral activities where the void never creeps up and there is no time for the contemplation of emptiness, or the ever-restless and haunted pursuit of wisps of vision? The happy or the haunted?

LUCY OLIVER

Sunday 19th May 1974

Spring, and the air is thick with wallflower and other perfumes mixing and seeping. I have just been perched on the bridge by the House-on-the-water and Magdalen Deer Park, but then I decided to come home since I could see no reason either to stay or go. The late afternoon was full of tourists peering.

I start my new job at the Nursery tomorrow.

T and I went down to London last Thursday to vote at Australia House. (Whitlam back with a narrow majority it seems.) After dinner in a French restaurant in Soho, a play, and a walk along Kensington High Street, I caught a bus to meet Mary (*sister*) at Swiss Cottage. I left her for the last time before she leaves England, standing on a street corner, the children hopping up and down impatiently. I shall greatly miss Mary and Ken. We had a lovely dinner with T when they were in Oxford a week ago; it was nice to be friends with relations!

I'm seeing a great deal of T. Every now and then I issue a 'Warning' in some fashion, but mostly I'm very glad to be affectionate (and idiotic). He continually disarms me by facing the truth about himself with his odd gentle humility.

A little nagging worry disturbs me about the nature of loving. Does 'growing to love' someone mean that gradually, by dint of constant association and affection for the good times, one comes to love these things so that the initial (and still present) incompatibilities come to matter less? If so, I don't like it. It is not how I want to love. It frightens me because it can grow and have power, perhaps the power of habit.

I came home from London sad and tense after leaving my family and called for T. He came, comforted my tears and took me out into the warm night near Binsey. How can one not feel affection and gratitude for one who answers needs like this?

Last night we went out to the Trout at Godstow. Rather marvellous under the lime-green trees as the waters raced and peacocks cried from the roof and trees overhead. A magnificent male peacock took off from the roofs, narrowly missed T's Guinness, and perched above the water on a derelict bridge of boughs. There, dead centre, he remained, crying out occasionally above the low milling of people, drinks and smoke.

T talked about his family. I said little but uttered feeble female chatter occasionally. What's happened to me!? Lost grit, guts, will, determination and sense of purpose. Can't think.

Last weekend my old friend O came to Oxford. We had a pleasant day on the river with T and P. The highlight for me occurred as we navigated the rollers which released our punt into the water. The punt slowly started its downward journey, pushed by four pairs of hands, when suddenly I grabbed O and we jumped in together. Instantly we gathered speed, and the brilliant red prow of our punt hit the water with a mighty splash, and with both shock and glee, the two of us shot off down the river, laughing hysterically.

T & P were left simply gazing after us in astonishment, holding the pole!

Wednesday 22nd May 1974

Preparing for another domestic evening reading and listening to Verdi Requiem. I'm having many of these evenings now, quite a contrast to last term.

But there are several things on which I must make a stand. I must tidy up my sloppy attitude to T which is pure laziness and an unwillingness to face the future. Instead of discussing things seriously with him, I simply giggle and produce a jumble of half-statements and irrelevancies. Asking whether I would consider living with him and making a future, as he has a couple of times, reveals a different train of thought from my own, and more affection and commitment than I could ever offer to him. I tried to stutter out my position, expectations and ideals etc, but then I cling closer and bury myself in the warmth of the present moment. Don't actions speak louder than words? (Though the words are truer than the actions.)

Wake up, girl! I have the consistency of protoplasm, and the same colour and modus vivendi.

Teaching has already been good for me. I felt alive today, felt useful, needed, with emotions waking up with the vulnerability of the responsibility and isolation of the teacher's role.

I had taken a job assisting in a nursery school dealing with tiny tots—not my secondary training, but a lovely occupation in this semi-unsettled phase of life.

My maternal instincts are very strong these days! I made friends with my favourite child today and felt great happiness in winning a communication from her shy but sturdy little personality. She won my heart the minute I saw her, delicate and shy, but contained and intelligent, and delicate as porcelain she appears. There are several others I have warmed to immediately, and a couple whom I shudder to see in the clumsy hands of nice, well-meaning but stereotyped teachers. Children with problems treated simply as 'naughty' or 'devils' to be castigated over and over again and told what sort of children they *are*. Children literally shaking with frustration, anger or unhappiness for being clumsy. I was surprised to see such obvious psychology-book examples treated with such old-fashioned rigidity.

CHAPTER 5
Choice and Consequence

―――

Thursday 29th May 1974

Eights Week. *(Annual inter-collegiate Regatta)* I am official Organizer of Teas for Magdalen Boat Club, a very pleasant activity when out of work in lovely weather. Hours of sandwich-making this morning; lunch at Magdalen, then punting our crockery and sandwiches down the Cherwell from Magdalen Bridge to the Boathouses.

This was very colourful: P & M in the first boat were in brilliant crimson blazers, bow-ties and white flannels, and pushing a red punt laden with provisions down the sparkling river. The trees seemed extra-green, and Magdalen tower was sharp against the sky. I was draped languidly over the prow, glad to be a necessary part of the spectacle, this traditional historical pageantry of Oxford.

The banks of the river were alive with people down by the boathouses. 'Young gentlemen' came seeking refreshment. Arrogant and charming, they paid out little tickets for the sandwiches and occasionally drank the poisonous tea.

Monday 3rd June 1974

Six pm sounding on the Meadow bells. Yellow flowers in the long grass and the field still with long shadows and pecking birds. I sit in some confusion, reviewing the events of the weekend. Just came from school. Not a smooth day, so tired and not buoyant.

Saturday, last day of the Eights, was exhausting. An augmented team of sandwich-cutters swung into action at 10.30 am, after my usual tussle with the shops getting supplies. We loaded the punt and floated down the dappled river. Festivity in the air with sweeping skirts and hats, blazers blooming, banks thronging with socializing multitudes.

I almost cracked under the rush but managed to maintain a fixed smile as I poured vast quantities of dubious tea into grubby cups. At last, thank God, teacups and food ran out, and I abandoned shop. With the booty slung over my shoulder, I met up with some others, and a dark strange dust-storm blew up the river as we watched the first division at 6pm.

Returned by punt to Magdalen to join a party under the colonnades of New Building, drinking white wine under the wisteria, with a purple sky behind the pinnacles, and thinking of C.S Lewis who lived and wrote in this building.

Then we adjourned to another party across the High where we drank champagne until the small hours. I was fascinated by a Spanish Count, all debonair and drooping; amused by the pleasant wholesome lads of the 1st Division, and by a talented magician; and exasperated by an awful Armenian who ended the evening following me around like a poodle. I finally left about 3 am.

However, while I was thus enjoying myself and flirting with others, T had received the news of his father's death. Manifold repercussions. He had waited in vain sitting in the car for me to return from my carousing on Saturday night, then came round early on Sunday morning. Quite a shock. Visions of an immediate and permanent return to Australia made me realize how much I'd miss him. All plans for the summer cancelled of course. He'll be leaving immediately after the exams in 4 weeks, and he asked me if I would return with him.

As we strolled through the tunnel of Addison's Walks, he asked me to marry him. I was thrown off balance by this proposal. Although I know it is out of the question and would be disastrous in the long run, yet it is perturbing in its possibility and deeply touching. My affection for him is naturally increased, yet I could not consider marriage. And not yet. Not now.

Imagine: all the forces of restlessness, anticipation, questing, and future which drive me on and keep me alive, just *stopped*! Not in resolution, the beginning of a vast new work of creation as exciting and relentless as previous forces; but just stopped mid-stream. With one decision, the rest of my life charted and settled.

It would be just for the sake of being settled. And for affection.

But it is not enough. Above all not enough for T who deserves more than a life-destroying compromise when there is even no need. I have much time yet to retain my ideals of marriage and to quest for the great Beginning. When it becomes unlikely, then will be the occasion for a calm bond of affection and settling together with someone. Hope T can see it this way. I can't imagine that he could see in me the absolute end of his road, the vital sparking that I still seek. Perhaps his urge is for settling, steadiness and a life-pattern. He is a bit older and closer to disillusion than I, and he needs someone so! Would that I could help!

As his time for departure draws closer, I fear I will begin to cling. A bad time to leave when we stand to miss each other most, and are most likely to magnify and distort emotions. Both entering a vacuum. I must be strong, and not crucify him for the weakness of an immediate need, for his affection is probably stronger. We are absolutely not suited. Don't forget it.

Tuesday 4th June 1974

Heard Lord Kenneth Clark reminiscing and reading poetry in the Union tonight. Evening sun on bookcases, brown chairs and ticking clock above the old Arts man, as he peered above his glasses and talked of Yeats, Dylan Thomas, E M Forster, Auden, Graves and other figures of eminence he has known. TS Eliot, Churchill too. He read in his rambling voice as birdsong blew in the open windows. He has cultivated the harmless eccentricities and privileges of an eminent man—speaking his mind with charm, as if *performing* humanity, just in case we conceive of him in marble.

I loved hearing of those I love.

But the 'civilization' in that pompous place was a little syrupy. Adjourned to the bar with P and two friends; literati for once.

Sunday June 9th 1974

Sundays have the texture of a baby's bottom.

I have sat here all afternoon, combing over memories and images, flicking through thoughts and filing my finger-nails, and consuming all the lard of the Sunday Times with lethargic absorption.

The weather alternates between sun and hail. It's safer to be indoors behind my Mateus bottle heavy with two orange blown roses. The Botanic Gardens are draped with a great load of roses, and the perfume gathers in clumps. I think summer is dignified by its roses. Even in rain and cold they cling grimly to its identity: the 'Season of Summer'.

My interior life has dried up. This is the cause of a pervasive dissatisfaction out of keeping with the contented surface of my world. Already I feel like a fag-end; as if all the energy and potential I once possessed has been mis-directed or ignored, talents dissipated. A middle-aged emptiness at 23! Oh woe! Living from one diversion to the next party or film. It's so easy to end up like this, a feeling of self-disappointment. What massive and healthy burst of energy is needed to blow the wholesome breezes of activity through a constipated system? Sounds despicable anyway!

I think of moments of community with T, eg, strolling by the canal in the evening sunshine, all togged up in black and white to attend a cocktail party in Jericho. The greening river, talking of Carlton, arm in arm. Community, but not intimacy of mind or spirit. When he leaves, taking the structuring out of my life, taking his soft hair and warmth, what then? We're like a badly synchronised watch, occasionally moving together, but usually in ungainly bobs. Even for this, these moments of shared grotesquery, I grow fonder.

Sunday 15th June 1974

The Parks, 6pm. The sun has just gone behind a cloud after a hot day, so now it is warm and still, all roses and humidity. Black and white figures are striding home from exams in sub-fusc. There are women in long full skirts (the Laura Ashley romantic revolution in dress) pushing prams.

I've shopped most of the day after leaving T's this morning through the summery streets and trees of north Oxford. At the Carpenter's Arms last night, T was jaded after a day of exams, and present also was that well-known anthropologist whom I still regard with silent wariness. The unexpectedness of the man; the childish eccentric games and long-winded anecdotes, suddenly dropping to reveal a most penetrating grasp of the situation. The alcoholic haze is but a mask. I feel stupid, dull and annoyed at my stolidity. Perhaps it is after all my personality, and the excuse of waiting for a 'properly congenial' environment to spark me into life again is becoming pretty limp. Was I always so awkward and unimaginative?

DD joined us in the pub. His wit and active perspicacity I find easier to handle, superficially. I am like a sponge, and have soaked in all the newness and different-ness of the 'motherland' and 'exotic' Europe with a sort of awe, and have not yet been able to give out anything at all. Is there anything to give? I feel so meagre, so dry and empty in comparison with the richness and subtlety of this Old World.

We ended over whisky at N's, and the anxious evening was somehow made worthwhile when he produced some old books and made me read aloud from the first editions: bits of Butlers 'Hudibras', and 'The South Sea Bubble Company' by Swift. Stumbling over the unfamiliar ſ's and whisky fumes, the words, the wit, the poetry were actually alive, and I felt them more trustworthy than the shifting states and people around.

Reading Vera Brittain's *Testament of Youth*. Wading through the prim sentimentality and earnestness, but dimly moved. I feel I *ought* to read it, I who know the corpulent lassitude and security of an easy peace. How far we have forgotten the anguish and striving of those years. I almost envy her the sharpness of pain, the vividness of death in life, and life in death. I, whose emotions are about as lively as a river of treacle.

I find it difficult to enter even imaginatively into her losses, because I can't think of anyone to whom I could give the role of dying who would stir up any vaguely equivalent emotions in me.

I think Vera Brittain has been good for me though, not only in seeing how many losses a human being can be dealt and live, but in her intelligent and committed feminism. Difficult to discern whether her intellect is, in fact, of the standard she fondly believed it to be, but yet the combination of femininity with a determined dedication to the life of the mind, is a thorn in my conscience.

I will arise and go now, not to Innisfree, but discarding this soft decadence of romantic sensibility, to......where??

Wednesday 26th June 1974

I have returned from the 'Footlights' Revue, which was superb in parts, eg, the meeting of the Paranoics Society; the obituary for an actor who was 'so self-effacing he was a great Hamlet and an even greater Godot'; the existentialist railway man who left all points open and created a multiple track pile-up.

I went with DS, who was also the cause of a pleasant evening last week at a University College concert at Lord and Lady Redcliffe-Maud's 'little pad' there. I shall never forget Lady Redcliffe-Maud playing Chopin on her grand piano. How beautiful she was—60 or even 70 years old perhaps, but so beautiful and strong as she played.

(She was exactly 70 at this time, and was a professional pianist.)

I was so inspired that when in a fit of boredom, I took out a lump of clay which had been mouldering in my wardrobe, it was her face which took shape. How very much a person in her own right she seemed, not a fluttering 'other-half', but someone who has worked out her destiny.

What else have I done? London last Saturday and the usual pattern of wandering, theatre and dinner. At the National Gallery the Ruben's turned me on a little.

The rest of the week is to be a heavy round of party-going. The day of T's departure is drawing closer; I shall probably be with him constantly until then, so if we don't bore each other to death, the parting will probably be quite a wrench. I've decided it is a good thing he's going, and if we do see too much of each other this week. It could never work long-term, but could have drifted on indefinitely in a familiar, non-strained way.

Sunday 30th June 1974

Oh, this hideous weather! Another grey rainy Sunday after a whole week of rain and bleakness. My spirits rose momentarily with a gleam of sun yesterday. Why am I such a weather-cock? Can I not be independent of my environment, or is there nothing to stand alone?

And having no control over my emotions. It has been a difficult week; all these parties—not happy occasions. My ambivalent feelings towards T, a mixture of genuine affection, sometimes impatience, clinging then disgust at it, and a poignant sensation of having destroyed the clarity of his affection for me; the warmth seems to have gone. All idiotics! I couldn't respect dogged devotion, and try it sorely, but am miserable when I succeed! It is the sense of being unfair, of shame which is upsetting me most. Why do affairs of the heart end with sadness and whimpering?

Later.

Well, it's not been a good day. Another contribution to the shadowiness that makes up the under-layer of living! Now I've pulled the curtain and am huddled under a lamp in my cellule, the real world has receded. The spotty English day, the twitching trees, the solid figures—all the things that pluck at the emotional centres of real existence have been vapourised. Only Imagination roves!

T takes on mythical status in his absence. What frightens me about loving is that it might sneak up from behind, slip in the back door, and be there before one can protest. I've always believed that Love, with a capital C for commitment, would be fairly obvious from the start, and then one could watch it grow and expand with time.

But is it so? What if it creeps up like a fog around clear incompatibilities and obfuscates them by creating its own environment and setting up its own warm and demanding patterns? If so, is it *Real*? Would it last, or suddenly dissolve when some original and forgotten strands of personality reasserted itself later? Am I ignoring something real? T and I have similar life-styles, taste in friends, common background, but not similar preoccupations. All my religious-y, mystical, philosophical, poetical leanings are mere matters of intellect to T. He operates on quite a different plane.

Tuesday 2nd July 1974

So, T has gone. At present I feel utterly miserable. It's raining of course.

I see nothing clearly. Nothing.

Have I done right, sending him away when once I could have gone with him? I expect so, but now in the confused pain of parting, only love is uppermost. When he said that on his return it would be better not to resume where we left off, I agreed, but with such a shot of pain. God, I shall miss him.

Later. A long chat with Dn helped me over the worst. I cannot conceive how anyone could survive grief without other people's help. How anyone could survive a really tragic bereavement utterly confounds my imagination. What does one do with pain when there are no sympathetic people to distract one's mind from the naked source? Snuff out, surely.

Dramatic, but I missed T with such overwhelming force, compounded with confusion and regret that it was awful. Talking puts the situation at second remove, as does writing. I would never have foreseen that T would be the cause of so much anguish, and much of it from a feeling of having been insufficiently sensitive to his emotions over father and home. Sorry T. So sorry.

Then Rn came over and cheered me up greatly with his chatter and energy.

Wednesday 10th July 1974

A quote by Aldous Huxley on the death of Maria Huxley:

" She knew what love was, had been capable of love as few human beings are capable. Now she must go forward into love, must permit herself to be carried into love, deeper and deeper into it, so that at last she would be capable of loving as God loves—of loving everything, infinitely, without judging, without condemning, without either craving or abhorring."

How can I understand these things so well—yet not? I know about them, but cannot *realize* them. What is the process of realization?

I am fascinated by the idea of erotic love. Love and eroticism have never been combined in my experience; I cannot imagine what it must be like. I dimly hold to the ideal that it must be marvellous!

Saturday 20th July 1974

Twelve after midnight. Just walked from the station through the dirty streets, cracked and oily paving stones, the weedy, platform-soled youths, and the silence of a warmish night.

I scurried gratefully into my burrow. Oxford at night, with its treasures locked up (including students) is sullen and grimy.

London, when I left it at Piccadilly, was solid movement and colour. Once upon a time, nights were nights. For all those millennia of human living, darkness was half their lives. Now it is relegated to the interstices between neon and bulbs. No wonder we have lost the powers of darkness, ie. not evil, but those which flourish in silence and darkness: the underneath of the conscious mind, the indefinable.

I saw 'Flowers', a mime by Lindsay Kemp as tribute to Jean Genet. All those images of horror and evil! There isn't any in my life, so I almost dismissed the white vampirish figures dripping blood as lurid gothic symbols occurring most readily to adolescents. But then, existentialism is an adolescent literature, though no less important for that. That my life does not have blood-stained teeth is no denial that they exist!

There is horror around. It is in every sterile gesture and life-denying action, gentle cruelties, indulgence, selfishness, narrowness et al.

CHAPTER 6
The Journeys of Summer

———

Wednesday 31st July 1974 Entre Paris et Firenze

Left Paris this afternoon. What a beautiful city! I am quite in love with the broad trees and dappled avenues of colour of this leisurely, human and alive city.

Yesterday I met Kathy at the tomb of Oscar Wilde in Pere Lachaise, by an extraordinary Egyptian monument by Epstein. This ancient cimetière, with its hills of stone, marble and trees, is cool and green and quiet in the heat of a summer day. I stood by Heloise and Abelard's gothic memorial, and peered through rusted doors into the broken pots and cracked glass of tiny chapels, apartments in miniature in a suburb for the dead.

We also spent a whole day at Chartres, keeping tryst with the blue light in that incomparable cathedral.

Alone again, I'm writing on the train to Florence, and am hot, and conditions are difficult. The horrible confusions I experienced with Student Travel reached a lovely conclusion in allocating me a wagon-lit on an Express to the beautiful Italian city. However, during an excellent meal in the dining-car, strange noises could be heard beneath the coach. Turned out it had lost a wheel! There followed an interesting delay in a tiny station in the southern part of France, in which little men on bicycles cycled up and down the train. The night was warm and still, with a large moon riding over quiet stone streets. I rather enjoyed the unscheduled event. Now, speeding towards Firenze, I am about to sleep.

Thursday 8th August 1974 Firenze

It is an inferno here! After a week I feel more adjusted to the climate and temper of this city, but still not in tune with it. A cradle of culture, birthing a new age in art—what, here?—where the streets are full of leering men, babbling people, noise, belligerence and dog-shit? Hard to credit, we are thinking, but have realised that 'sensitive types' must have deserted Firenze en masse, leaving it to Tourists and workers. It's a difficult place for an Anglo-saxon! I'm so tired of being constantly molested. I tried to sit in the Boboli Gardens to study Italian, but it was hopeless. I was approached twice in the space of ten minutes!

The city is lovely at night, cool and quiet from a distance.

The Pensione is not very comfortable, but the people are enjoyable and we students get on well. However, I'm not ecstatically happy, and not even able to appreciate art properly because I'm too hot. My incentive to learn Italian is dwindling because I don't *want* to understand all the propositions and obscenities constantly assailing my ear! I feel vulnerable, and slightly uneasy.

Friday 9th August 1974

It's easier to cope when feeling more at ease. Sometimes it doesn't bother me now to walk down the street. Perhaps I'm adjusting. I enjoy the classes and our black-bearded teacher who conducts an adult gathering with charm and efficiency.

Earthquake last night was a notable event. Just as we were falling asleep there came a strange movement of the blind, then a noise and shaking which made B and I sit up in horror and shock. I wrapped a cover round my naked form and ventured into the corridor where no one seemed disturbed. In the morning, others had felt it, but most had noticed nothing and frankly disbelieved our stories! Only a radio report of earthquake saved our reputations.

And the resignation of President Nixon was announced: 'Nixon si dimette'. The entire Watergate saga is difficult to accept as real, and the extraordinary tenacity of Nixon above all. I am convinced he cannot be sane in the ordinary sense of the word, or is it the product of a culture utterly amoral and mechanically working towards programmed goals of self-gain and material individual aggrandisement? It's not that I didn't know intellectually and expect this sort of activity, I just never expected to see it revealed so concretely and incontrovertibly! The scale and degree of the corruption is staggering, and the implications and reverberations mind-boggling.

Thursday 15th August 1974

Giorno Festivo, and Florence is handed over to Tourists. With N,C and B we walked miles from Piazza Michelangelo looking for trees and grass. Vain hope. Beautiful trees and grass were in evidence, but all behind huge walls. Not an accommodating city!

Every so often, when doing my duty in Church or Museum, something moves me particularly. Surrounded by so much High Renaissance art, it is usually the pre-renaissance which evokes a response in me. I admire, but find no mystery, no room for imagination and its poetry in the glories of the Renaissance; the magnification of man and his works, constant rejoicing in new intellectual discoveries. Rather it will be some tiny panel under a larger gilt altar-panel which jolts my apathy, like the journey into Egypt surrounded by gilt, three calm humble figures and a dark grey donkey emerging from a strange dark wood and pattern of trees, filled with mystery and pathos. This was in S. Trinita this afternoon, as was a nativity by Ghirlandao I loved, with three shepherds whose faces are so finely etched.

Dined in Fiesole with the school, after watching Fellini's 8½. Good to see in location amid the contradictions of Italy. Was sorry I couldn't understand the conclusions enunciated at the end.

Saturday 24th August 1974 Vinci

Here in Vinci, by Leonardo's house, is one of the nicer moments in Italy, in the orchard stratified with olive trees and scattered with grape-vines, pear, fig and peach trees. We settled under a spreading fig, and R returned with a bunch of purple grapes for our lunch.

Has Leonardo lain so, under these broad green leaves which catch the sun and passing cloud? So near his house, in the hills and valleys steep with olives. It's a delicate day, cool with clouds over the summer sun and bursts of brilliance. Warm of course.

C,B,R and others chatter in German, jokes which P and I lying on our backs cannot understand. Yet it is still beautiful, the clamour of strange tongues in a strange country. We are all together, and all this strangeness so easily becomes familiar and part of oneself. We ate bread and cheese with wine and fruit, and meal over, with one accord we lay flat out on the prickly grass, pervaded by well-being.

From this hill there is a blue-green vista of distant mountains. I understand Leonardo's painting much better having seen the landscape of his youth, most fortunately not in the dead heat of a blazing afternoon, but on a misty day when the mountains are just the shade of blue behind the Madonna of the Rocks. Light streamed from behind clouds in almost aethereal beams. The chief feature of the landscape is light; very alive. Ragged, rocky formations of mountains familiar from his paintings, and overlapping edges of colour.

We marvelled at the virtuosity of his scientific imagination in the museum.

A wedding-party, gay and gaudy, wound its way up the sleepy streets. Italy at last as I wanted to see it, I thought!

Assisi

I love the organic nature of the villages, man-made avenues of stone, the romance of arches, walls pressing together, stairs setting off to....where? Alleys turning to invisible destinations; passageways open to imagination; geometry set in motion. Angles open and close, straight lines extend themselves and intersect with others; shadows in all their infinite gradations swim and confuse the edges of forms with the real lines of stone. Alternatively, one can just stand still for a long time, and the landscape changes colour and shapes from morning through to night.

Uffizi

Clothes must be God's greatest gift to artists! The swirling of an angel, all translucent and shimmering with colours; delicate flat folds of the straight, still figures in Ghirlando's frescos in Santa Maria Novella. No reproductions can ever capture the fine edges and delicate tones of the original. Glints of gold along the edges of a gown; a faint flush on the face of a Madonna; a tiny shadow at the corner of a mouth. All are lost.

Wednesday 28th August 1974

Rain from leaden skies and flickers of lightning over the Ponte Vecchio. It is unusual weather. Last night was spectacular as we stood on the bridge at midnight and watched the far-off flickers of the coming storm. Later, sleepless in bed, it broke.

(Italian courtyards are extraordinary places. All sounds are magnified; all neighbours share each other's lives, aurally if not visually! And they never seem to go to bed! Coughing, yells, creaks, bangs and sounds of activity and yowls of cats continue through the night.)

Stimulated in mind, and aware of all these noises, I lay there with the lightning flashing into the room. Then, with an eerie moan of wind and the slashing shut of a window, the rain began and thunder shook the houses. I got up for a marvellous view from the pensione window of high dilapidated roofs, shot with light. Rapt with currents of excitement at this spectacle, I didn't hear B get up until she was suddenly beside me, lightning on her face. I yelped with shock, and we both babbled with fear...

Saturday 31st August 1974 Roma

Today we strolled down the Appian Way, strange and dramatic. The narrow dusty road never deviated for so many miles; ruined lumps of marble among the long unkept grass and gnarled pine-trees. In afternoon sunlight, the fields stretched raggedly towards a hazy Roma. We spent the morning paddling through the ruins of Imperial grandeur, and lunched on panini and cheese on the top of the Palatine Hill.

We finished the day by a drive out to the lakes in misty evening light. Joined a Communist Fetta d'Unita—the faces of the children so beautiful. The fine things of travelling are the people and small towns when you are the only 'visitors' rather than tourists. And our evening meal in a small Osteria in the middle of nowhere and vineyards, which we could probably never find again. We were the only guests, part of the family. Over the remnants of a large bowl of purple grapes and fresh figs—picked from the tree less than an hour before—we smoked cigarettes and ventured into philosophy and linguistics, as is customary after a good meal. Never get far, but...!

Then to Roma centro, where the Trevi Fountain really was beautiful: great sheets of water over the marble, rough-hewn, with the bodies of horses and men rising from the rocks. I was surprised to find it in such a small intimate piazza, being used to Florence with its vast open piazzas.

Friday's most wonderful experience was a spur of the moment entry into the Coliseum late at night. Weird. It was imbued with presences. I could almost hear the roar of vanished crowds. The crumbling arches were lit, but full of shadows. We were all deeply moved, except P, who seemed unable to face the power and menace of the place. R, C and I sat for some time on the stones above the dark doorways from which lions must have entered, and speculated about history. I felt how strongly we are descendants of those who have gone; how in many senses they are still living, those vanished generations, through us. The brutality, lusts, passions and emotions spent in that place are very, very much alive. We are they, and they have life in us. The Past then, is sacred, per se.

Sunday 1st September 1974

After visiting St Peter's in the morning, and leaving in disgust from what was unmistakeably like Paddington Station, we headed for the coast. My first sight of the Mediterranean! Grey and choppy, a stiff wind tugging at my scarf, we found a beach with few people, and spent the afternoon lying in the sun, singing to R's guitar (Bella Ciao is the theme song of this trip). Unless I concentrated hard, I was swept far away to Fairhaven *(my coastal childhood.)* As I wandered alone by the sea-shore, it was the Me who had paddled long ago by that other distant ocean, dreaming of far-away places. Yet I was *here*, by the fabled Mediterranean on a beach near Rome, not much changed, yet so irrevocably older!

Wednesday 4th September 1974

Beautiful, beautiful Venice!

I arrived this afternoon about 5pm. The sun filtered through leaves onto the walls of buildings in small paved piazzas, through vines, arches and on the waters. It seemed so lovely.

I met K & J for dinner at a student trattoria, then caught a boat from Piazza San Marco to the Rialto. A large orange full moon hung over the lagoon, and lights made streaks across the black water. When I left the boat, my real pleasures began—walking and walking through tiny 'calle', over bridges, under arches, in absolute safety with no molesting at all. I felt elated. The piazza by the fish-market was fascinating, and I recognised it from a film set in Venice with Julie Christie, in which Venice was deserted because of plague. Here now, deserted this evening, were papers blowing round the font in that same square. The columns went down to the water, and there was a faint smell of fish.

Bridges and alleys seem to have no beginnings or end, but turn into each other. I could have walked forever in the cool night. It is a poetic city. Glimpses through windows of chandeliers, paintings, walls lined with books. An elegant and cultured city.

C and I had parted at Padua, she for Vincenza and I for Venezia. We had a tedious journey to Padua yesterday, on her 21st birthday, when the train halted just before Florence for 4 hours! Confined in the stalled train as if in a tin, we listened nervously to rumours of 'bombe' and 'alarme' (many people were killed by a fascist bomb on the same line a few weeks ago). Finally, at 3pm the train started to move. My heart was in my mouth a little as we immediately entered a long tunnel. Reading today's paper we found out that a huge quantity of dynamite and a large hole was found near the railway line. It seems we were quite close to destruction!

Tuesday 10th September 1974 Zermatt

Switzerland, under that most compelling Alpine symbol, the Matterhorn. Almost sadly, even this untouchable has lost its remoteness for me—I've invaded it and know it, from walking all day on the high Alpine pastures, past the tiny hamlet of Zmutt to

Kalbermatter. I lay in the sun and with my head on the soft pillow of my handbag, and watched the clouds court the mountain-peak, until by the middle of the afternoon, it stood free and proud against the gentian sky, and so remained until the sun set.

As I climbed the rocky path towards the summit, I passed walkers shod in hiking boots with sticks and backpacks. Yet, I in my sandals, was not disgraced, and I reached quite an altitude! It was a dream come true, and if only the weather holds, tomorrow promises another expedition. The softness of milk chocolate on the tongue (so necessary for energy!); the bells of sheep moving on high pastures; the play of clouds on snowy peaks; warm sun in cool Alpine air.

After arriving at Lugarno on Friday, P and I went for a drive over the Furke Pass and St Gotthard. This, my first real view of the Alps, decided me where I'd spend the next few days: the Matterhorn beckoned irresistibly! We went inside the Rhone Glacier, blue and freezing, from which the mighty Rhone sprang in a small trickle down the valley, and walked for hours above the village of Andermatt to watch the sun set in great streaks of crimson cloud.

I'm feeding off splendid sights, but now sort of enjoying being alone.

Thursday 12th September 1974

How sorry I will be to leave this beauty. Each of my three days has been an idyll, and today Sunnegga: a white and blue Matterhorn and roars from the waterfall across the valley. And that glass of beer after the stiffest, hottest climb I've made—I thought I'd never taste water again! However, the view from the top made all striving worthwhile. I'd forgotten to eat lunch, so sat under a larch and ate salami and rye bread at 3.30, blissfully content, reading Nietzsche.

A blue haze hung in the valley all afternoon, which deepened as the sun grew lower, and streaks of light emanated from all the peaks towards the sinking sun. A field of snow near the Matterhorn shone pristine and polished, like the last launch-pad to the ethereal regions, and the mountains were layered in blue, each edge sculptured against its background.

Two old women sitting on a bench replied to my greeting, "Oh, you walk so nice!" No compliment could have made me happier! As it happened, I had just drunk a beer with peanuts and the road was broad and flat, so no wonder my step was light and rhythmic! But I guess that in contrast to the trudge of weary mortals in hiking boots with rucksacks, in my blue jeans and sandals, light top and shoulder-bag, I must have looked very carefree!

In the morning it was forest. Up through the larch woods the sun lay in fresh green pools among the grass and rocks. It was so still—frozen light, and seemed the ultimate statement of stillness and completeness. A statement of itself; no more. I was reminded both of eternal childhood and of tombs. Youth and death. This afternoon I noted particularly the sun through a patch of tall delicate grasses, red-stemmed and shining, so that it seemed the sun itself which orchestrated their movement.

In the valley of Findhelm, which is a typical Swiss hamlet of brown wooden houses, there was a veritable symphony of bells. Sheep produced a high-pitched cacophony on one side, and three beautiful Jersey cows chimed in from the other with deep tones.

Two tiny new-born lambs cuddled each other by the road. A jersey cow wandered up, and appeared quite concerned at their bereft state. She studied and licked them, and went on her way, but they tottered after her on skinny black-tipped legs—unmistakeably ballet-shoes!

That was today's nature study!

Yesterday I took a cable car to Trockener Weg, where winds and clouds blew across the snowfields. It was cold and strange. The mountains do roar. I set off downhill bravely in my sandals through the barren rocks and ice. Zermatt 3½ hours said the sign. By afternoon though, I was happily meditating as I reached the lower pastures.

Always in the background of these travels in Europe that summer, was the decision I made to part with T and decline the life he offered to me. This day, on the high pastures, I really tackled the question, and tried to find some peace with it. I did not regret it, but something shifted.

I don't want to leave, but I fear that to stay after this blessed time would be to try for two bites of the apple! Better to keep the memories. I love the people here: always the greetings "Grüß Gott" or "Grüße Sie", as husband and wife set off it pairs, dressed similarly. I imagine them as a unity after many years of marriage, still openly affectionate, and somehow youthful. Slightly envious seeing them, and the beautiful blond children.

Which has made me reflect a lot on my current situation. What if I were to find complete and utter 'fulfilment' from a relationship, which is what I have always waited for? Wouldn't it be the end of the road? What then? A great blank? Nothing left to strive for, no edge of wanting-ness. Is not this vital restlessness and falling short of perfection essential for growth and creativity?

Or indeed, could not the ideal relationship be too demanding, too total and consuming, so that in fact I lose freedom? Whereas a marriage which enables one to give love and be loved, for companionship and a base, would not this be a door to greater freedom? There would still be room to seek for the great fulfilment in other ways, still room to encompass a lot of people with love. It wouldn't be a waste, would it?

It's never occurred to me before—I've always been waiting and waiting for someone around whom to harness my energies; for someone to 'make me'.

Stand on your own two feet!

If I do find that wise counsellor one instinctively looks for to guide the inner journey, probably better that it not be a husband! I've managed so far with books and meditation. I can stand up by myself, even if sometimes it does get wearisome.

Reading Nietzsche has been good for me. If this attitude sticks when I get off this elevated mountainside, it will be a revolution in my thinking. Nietzsche insists on the necessity of standing alone, and on the recognition that we have bred a society of followers, trained to obey rather than initiate. The inner quest, though, must be one of rule and leadership—of oneself. The I Ching is addressed to Rulers and Leaders.

However, Nietzsche ended insane. He set himself a task, but broke in the process. It's dangerous. But quote: "Truth is dangerous." All was not well with the man behind the mind: a difficult personality and emotional needs unsatisfied.

Wednesday 18th September 1974

Sitting at a window in Venice again, but fighting waves of depression. After so long abroad, I simply want to go 'home', wherever that may be. Even Venice today was hot and crowded, smelly and dirty. My eyes could find no charm. I see the water now, dark and littered with papers. The pigeons on the building opposite are intermittently snapping, but preparing for sleep with heads tucked in. Loathe pigeons.

I feel so tired, of moving, of Italy.

Saturday 21st September 1974

Only a few more hours to fill before the train leaves for Vienna. Actually, it has all turned out very well. I met H, yet another Viennese girl on Thursday morning as I sat at breakfast in the little café opposite the hostel. She is quiet but strong and definite. We met for a protracted lunch on Murano Island, sitting outside under vines discussing the birth of her baby which is due round about my birthday next month. Very resolute is she, at 20, awaiting the birth of a child without marriage. As a student and so young, she knows the time has not come for marriage, though she seems to have a strong relationship with her boyfriend. It was good to talk with her about the themes preoccupying me now: femininity and independence, marriage etc., as we sat over ice-cream and cigarettes above the dark water one night.

I went to see the Peggy Guggenheim Collection of modern art, and really enjoyed it. All my favourites: Chagall, Dali, Ernst, Picasso and Miro, and beautiful sculptures scattered where they look so fine among the leaves and paving stones in the garden. Above all I loved the golden Brancusi, delicate arrows transfixed. Giacometti, very touching and lovely.

Often I think visual art is much finer than the word. So directly can one's soul and consciousness respond, the mind rests.

There I met an Australian minister for Education and Art, which led to luxurious dinner at the Gritti Palace on the Grand Canal. He was oh so Australian! He had the naivety of a student just left school and first beginning to think. He used me as a sounding-board for his ideas. So nice, so well-intentioned, but gauche and awkward. I think sophistication is not just perversion of innocence, but essential to maturity and balance of mind and judgement, and therefore of communication. Nuance and subtlety, and the ability to detach oneself from one's emotions, and achieve the synthesis of different propositions. Intelligent but unsophisticated was my judgement of our Minister, like many Australians.

Monday September 30th 1974

Waiting in the train from Vienna to London. I've just left C and her mother. How kind they have been! Tosca at the Opera from a red velvet box where I felt so elegant! The luxuriousness of the Opera House, and being part of it with C and G, both so good-looking an elegant. It was like being in a play myself. And the sauna with C was an enlightening experience. The freedom of nakedness, and how the women, old, or fat, were yet so feminine somehow, and even beautiful.

And last night a development in relationship with G. It was inevitable as during the course of the week, I found his attractiveness, openness and charm fascinating, and also the contrasts between C and G, *(sister and brother)* so alike, yet one so female and one so male. G and I eyed each other warily until last night, when with great sensitivity and courage, he recognised the moment, and it was a joy, a real happiness to embrace. We could speak of things which can only be spoken by a man and woman when very close. It's strange how all the doors of communication seem open and words come alive. He is young and so open; always graceful even when most unsure and afraid. I hope I have given him something as he has to me.

Later

Back in Oxford, and inevitably very dislocated. My room so familiar, yet somehow empty. No word from T.

I feel I want to phone anyone I know, but it's too late. Especially G. Isn't it strange, why he? Just because he is male. But now I am alone.

Friday 4th October 1974

Well, it's back to base one. Meeting with T last night was sad and painful. It's definitely over now. I feel very alone and have been busy today making new plans. I knew it would happen, but wish it has not been so (typically) graceless. When I saw him again, I wondered if there was any basis for attraction apart from the Past, but what iron chains this past history wields! As the night drew on, it was the old familiar situation again, the T I had come to depend on, and it was hard to accept that it was different.

So it was a bad night and morning again.

I feel better now, and even resolved to go on getting involved, because I believe that deadness or a shield against emotion is anti-life.

But I've let go of T. The world's spaces are blowing around me again and it's very cold. I must believe in warmth; that sometime this wind will cease; this tearing at the heart' places with icy slivers of wind that leave no sheltered corners.

I am alone, but free. I must go on.

Tuesday 8th October 1974

A bright Autumn day at last. Watched the deer again, the sun brilliant on the grass and dripping through the yellow trees along Magdalen Walks. I love these things, but I can leave them. This at least, and at last, I have learnt.

I met T and we had coffee together. I feel so free now. So obvious to me now, that we are insanely incompatible, yet still I felt a friendly warmth and affection for him. I'm so glad there's no bitterness. He has given me so much

Friday 18th October 1974

Can it be that it is over, the long Waiting? It has gone from me! I have a vast feeling of spaciousness and freedom; of a long life to be lived and much to do. I am thinking in terms of years—like beads on a string for me to fill and use. It's exhilarating! Have I at last matured, become whole? I cannot explain this newness and security, of being a woman, a Person.

It has ripened this summer. The Italian experience, my long thoughts on marriage; the slow gestation of my relationship with T; the making of friends, and then the encounter with G. How important this was. It confirmed in one beautiful gesture my feeling of woman-ness, to be attractive and able to be loved. Nothing else could have so swept up all the threads searching and doubting and finding into one conclusion.

'It' will come because I am ready. I have wasted enough time. Perhaps I have 'It' already. I feel that I have everything, that I am complete, and now life can get underway. Isn't it strange!

Saturday 19th October 1974

Reading Chinese poetry. Immensely consoling, these voices from so long ago, so direct and immediate, they vibrate with the emotions of life. How can I ever feel alone in grief when so many have stood by rainy windows, watched flowers in falling rivers, watched through the long beating hours of the night, and felt the Autumn gold and death as a force in their being?

The women particularly move me: the power and simplicity of their sorrows and joys. The vibrancy and poignancy of life. Always the rain in the background, and the ever-recurring Autumn, and how these reflect the internal moods and catch us up into the rhythms of the universe.

The treasuring of moments of love—common! Common to us all, the memory of gentleness, and darkness on limbs that grow and wind like trees.

Why must I live through it all again, when so many have done and felt and discovered and died, and their wisdom gone to ashes? What can I possibly learn that is new? The wisdom acquired at such cost, such searching through the years—it's been found so often before, and lost again. And I too, shall scramble through the briars, only to die, and have it all cast on the wind and utterly lost!

Yes? Yes!

Thursday 24th October 1974

Spent a fine day in London yesterday. Jumped off the coach in Kensington High Street where I at last found a coat I like, all grey and well-cut. Wearing my purchase (and admiring in all shop windows I passed), I set off for the Tate. It was a special exhibition: some marvellous Picasso and Klee. I identify very strongly with Picasso; feel this is how I would paint if I were a genius and painter!

It's his versatility and largeness of range and technique which are so fascinating, and the command of a sophisticated intelligence. Intellectual and intense, and have concentration, the quality so lacking in much modern art; to be long pondered.

After the exhibition I walked along the Embankment. The wind whipped the grey Thames with its load of vessels and stirred the great piles and carpets of leaves underfoot. Wonderfully Autumn; soft and crackling. It is the loveliest part of London; the London I will remember for its beauty.

I feel very at peace these days. I feel I have begun a new life, somehow am quite a new person. I have the rest of my life now to give from these years of accumulation and gestation. If I spend a year teaching English language in a foreign culture, that will be vital experience. So, my life has a purpose and I have a role. And I have Time: there is no haste.

Monday 11th November 1974

4pm and the sun's setting is a brief moment of charm for the Iffley Road. I've not been out all day, except for a trip to the laundromat, which is a bad thing, as my thoughts start milling round like a throng of company and take me over.

I've not been sleeping well. Last night was very strange. A high gusty wind which I had not been consciously aware of during the evening, somehow got inside me. When I went to bed it was restless sleep, and a sudden start into consciousness from a vast roaring gust of wind, followed by a loud clang of dustbin lid. I was electrified with shock. Then more rattles of lids. One bin lay upside down rocking on its handles, the other was prostrate on the road. I tried to ignore them, but the rattles were ominous.

Finally, I rose, and with real fear of being possessed by the wind, the trees, and the absolutely deserted Iffley Road, I went out in my dressing-gown. It was very strange out there at 4am. Exhilarating too!

Sleep was better after that and a quiet read.

Wednesday 13th November 1974

I'll go mad here! Must get a job. For four days I've seen no one and done nothing but read, and was perfectly happy until tonight when my resistance cracked. I'm sitting around like an old grandmother! I feel like a caged lion. Can't sleep; every night is like a battle on the high seas. No wonder I dreamt last night I was going to bed in a boat!

What am I doing here, living alone in a place where I have created no life? I nearly escaped. I was so full of enthusiasm and hope for Germany; now it's just a stale taste at the back of my throat. I do not want to go to Germany. I am not learning German. What has happened, damn it? I so nearly escaped.

Thursday 14th November 1974

Went walking this morning and revised my opinion of the world's face. Up St Aldates from signing on, the sun was a white shining force which transfigured Christ Church. The Broad Walk was floating with small yellow leaves in constant motion from the gale-force winds, and the Meadows were shining. And spices. Was I dreaming the heavy sweet scent of spice and incense?

Down the lane from a thatched cottage came a man with a barrow. The sun was behind him; he was all touched with silver, in his hair, his shabby suit.

Yes, it was a fine morning!

I watched a long worm mould himself along the ground. "It's an ill worm that has no turning."

Thursday 21st November 1974

Life is so neutral, like the rain, not vindictive. I suppose it's I who expect there to be some logical pattern of continuity, linking daily events towards some desired end. Suddenly the pattern is not there, ruptured, and I realize it was never there, but in my mind.

The mire, the bog of my emotions and insides! I prefer not to peer in too closely at present or it might all come oozing lumpishly out in great waving strands of possibilities and rubbery hopes.

I dream of a life as intricate and unified as a gothic cathedral, clear in its aspirations, each pinnacle of achievement finely finished and pointed. And I am faced with—me. Just the uncontrolled stew which is me! Should I take it firmly by the forelock ("take the bull by the udders") and get my hand of artistry working as others have? I cannot.

If I possessed the indomitable will which could impose form on the world around me, I would be some other person, not the Lucy I have known all these years.

Monday 25th November 1974

It's a siege. These days following each other with the consistency of putty. Streaks of life when the blood sings from inside out, but then dissipate into the day and leaves one unchanged.

Like this morning. The brilliant autumn/winter sun and the flooded Magdalen Meadows. I walked through the waters and long spindly tunnels of path. Just me, the sun, the water, and my camera. I was utterly happy, golden as a piece of butter in that spreading, shining landscape. The deer were very still today. Only the sun moved through the black, webby branches, and an occasional squirrel. Apart from them, I was the only moving point in a still world.

Then I was sucked into the city. My mind moved with the buses and paperboys and market-sellers. I was absorbed here like a piece of paper.

I came home, and the long coma of the evening began. I read Shakespeare and Virginia Woolf, listened to the disembodied emotion of Tomkins and English choirboys. And now it's nine o'clock. Soon I shall go to bed and wake, crinkled, to my dressing-gown and coffee, and begin the slow rhythm of the next day with a book on Picasso.

And it will be night again, closing down outside my defensive curtains.

I have not grown one day older for two weeks. Here is the secret of eternal youth: mushrooms and cigarettes! And a tall, calm innerness quietly gliding across the surface of the days.

But will it ever end? When?

Wednesday 27th November 1974

The quality of woman-ness I find hard to come to terms with. I think that I know what I am, how I'm likely to react, what personality traits make up Me. Yet there is something else. There is something beyond my conscious control, driving me to despair, or to unannounced elations or longings. I can identify certain states of emotion which are not specifically Me, but more related to Woman, to the workings even of her body.

I cannot be fully mistress of myself when at the mercy of sudden eruptions of sentiment, provoked perhaps by nothing more substantial than a curled-up flower!

Tuesday 3rd December 1974

Back from the Meadows. Now at 5pm darkness is thoroughly established. I had watched it settling, intensifying like the smoke in the mild Autumn air. The black elms almost came to life and vibrated across the still grass, so clear and beautifully were they present. Milkiness behind; the smell of evening, and the last bird-songs, ecstatic and invisible.

The Dean of Christ Church passed, lifted his black hat from his 'noble roman' head and enquired after my present situation. An unequal exchange, as I can hardly ask how the Cathedral is coming along! But with exquisite courtesy, he lifted his hat and bowed once again. "Nice to see you," he said and glided nobly along the path by Merton wall.

Sometime later I followed and discovered the source of the smoke: smouldering piles of leaves. I stirred them up and blew on them so that flames danced against the now very dark air. I was loathe to leave, but warm lights were coming on in all the colleges. So calm. So rich. I almost wanted to scream and throw stones to crack the river and stir up all this peace!

I didn't. Went quietly home.

O came for the weekend and we dined luxuriously on fish and chips and beer in P's room in Magdalen. Took a late stroll around the Walks and found the gate locked when we returned. With considerable trepidation we each in turn climbed over the high wrought-iron gate and therefore could continue what turned out to be a very sociable evening!

CHAPTER 7
Alchemical Wedding

———

M*y life changed from this point, and a new process was set in motion.*

Wednesday 25th December 1974 Christmas Day

How can I assess this Christmas? Can I yet achieve any distance or make any statements? Or sort out the warm seething pool of emotions?

I am here in a village with O and her family and Kathy (*my sister*). A grey Christmas has passed with television and eating, and the hysterical hilarity of O's family. Now rain teems against the windows as I sit in a tiny study, rocking.

I am thinking, of course, of D. I am thinking of the last six days we have spent almost totally in each other's company; of how much has happened this week, how much changed, how much irrevocably. I feel both awe and a strange numb acceptance amounting almost to disbelief.

He is in my mind as he was the last night by the electric fire on the floor, his long knees folded under the black Prospero gown and his head questioning and rather beautiful with a Moses-like quality. I was curled up in a white cotton nightgown. I could watch the lace at my wrists and it too was beautiful. I felt the most complete and essential woman I have ever been. We were in the presence of archetypes. His vulnerability and my unfolding. It was a fine night—love and liver pate!

Who is this man whom I have so conquered without preamble? Whose full effect on me I have yet to determine? How can I accept so much from him...?

No—I cannot yet cope with understanding, or articulate. At this very moment I miss him, and the directness of the bond which is between us. I want saturation, yet fear its distortion and question its substance. But I suppose I have no choice. When we are together, it's totally.

It happened like this. A couple of weeks prior to Christmas 1974, I had dragged myself out of my snug abode to attend an event in town. Crossing Magdalen bridge in the darkness of an early winter evening, I became aware of something different: about me, about the air, about the winter apple tree by the bridge. An indefinable atmosphere, which I recalled later as somehow presaging something significant, as if I was slipping through a rent in the fabric of space-time.

It was the evening I encountered a tall rangy figure of a man, and something clicked into place.

Next day he insisted on accompanying me as I did my shopping in the Oxford covered market. The happening which tipped my world sideways was very slight, but dated from a long time ago, when as a child I had a dream which I conceived as an encounter with 'the man I would marry'. In the dream, a 'presence' came up behind me as I was crouched stroking the petals of a velvety pansy-flower in my garden, and he slipped his hand under my own, caressingly. I never saw his face in the dream, but felt his presence and quality so strongly that I was quite sure I would recognise him in reality, wherever and whenever He entered my life, and however far into the future it occurred. I stored the dream in some deep recess of my memory.

Suddenly the dream surfaced in the Oxford market, when I turned around and saw this man I had only just met caressing the petals of a velvet pansy on a stall in exactly the way I had seen in my dream long ago, and with just the same quality of presence.

The French word 'bouleversement' covers it best. It was an over-turning, a shock. The light changed; the scene changed and seemed to slip sideways; the fruit on the stalls glowed vivid orange. All I could think was: 'Him! 'Really? Someone in a dodgy grey parka with a furry hood? Someone who looks like that— long and odd, and not my type at all?'

But my heart melted within me.

And so, we got together. One of those first evenings he walked me home, and when we reached my door, under the trees and street-light, for the first time he bent and kissed me goodnight. It was gentle, warm, and totally seismic in effect on me. I made it up the steps and through the door, then plastered myself against the inside of the front door because my legs had ceased to function and my breath had almost stopped. I remained there for some time, bemused, and wondering what had happened. The cliché of romantic novels is not entirely a figure of speech!

Sunday 29th December 1974

Even winter in England sometimes has its glories! I set off at midday to Port Meadow. It was a brilliant lake in the low bright sun, edged in foam and white birds. A fierce wind stirred joy in the horses, which galloped—power and freedom incarnate—and took the narrow road in a leap, manes and tails flying. Later two came up to me and nuzzled my stomach, and I was able to lose my awe and stroke their matted fur. A brave deed for me!

Bossoms boatyard was teeming with life: children fishing from the bridge, swans, people working on bright boats on the brimming water.

Through Binsey and down the lane in streaks of sun. The church was musty and warm, draped in holly and candles. It is a little church very much possessing a God—a simple, seasonal God. I love to be there with the angel with the lute. Utterly still.

I shall like living near Port Meadow.

At this point I had moved from the Iffley Road to the other side of the town, into a tiny room in a shared flat up the Woodstock Road. There D would come, loping up the road from his book-lined room near the centre when I returned from work each day. I had left the nursery school and taken a proper teaching job at a Comprehensive school outside Oxford. This was a challenging placement, with a longish commute, and as things turned out, an enormous struggle for me.

Last Sunday D and I went together to Port Meadow, late as the sun prepared to set over mists and water. It was very cold, and a fire burned near the boats. We were drawn to its heat and colour and stood soaking in the light and wings of flame.

It was so nice to be there with D.

He belongs, even with the horses.

We stood together for a long time in common warmth as the sun set and a last bird sang.

Sunday 5th January 1975

Another Sunday in Port Meadow! A most absorbing place. Today all pearled, with milky water and trees, fishermen by the river, and a cloud of white birds swooping and playing with the water surface. Riveting!

From this point on my diaries become spasmodic for several months. Even now as I write forty-eight years later, tears have come to my eyes, and I am going to find it difficult to re-live a time so formative, so transformative. It was an initiation, a catalyst for change. When I began writing more consistently again, a new phase of life was beginning.

A month passed with no entries. I had entered into my own Valhalla. I cannot believe it was just a month, but intensity distorts time. I was sick, and so tired, my speech had dried up when I returned in a state of exhaustion and sickness from my teaching, but I was determined not to let feebleness and physical matters alter anything, and would sit across from D in the evenings watching him with quiet contentment, seeing us as a domestic couple reading together as we would down the years. One time I realized that I had been holding my book upside down all evening! I hoped he hadn't noticed, because I had been propping my eyes open by sheer force of will, and dissembling.

Until the blow fell. He revealed that he had noticed something had changed, and seared me with the words, gently spoken: "You're not the woman I fell in love with."

I was stupefied, paralysed. Who was I then? Who had he fallen in love with? Some image? Who or what is 'Me-I', that he should have missed it? Coming from a man of his discernment it was an existential assault which dominated my internal horizon for many months, and indeed touches on the profound question of ultimate identity. I was precipitated into this arena before I had the metaphysical equipment to deal with it, so I will edit out some of the wrestling with fundamental angst, analysis of male and female roles and psyche which pre-occupied my writing for the next few months when I picked up my pen. The relationship with D slowly ground down, and ground me down. My confused meanderings were without focus or resolution.

Resolution came later. The alchemical analogy of a refiner's fire is apt. Fire melts down raw materials, and fuses new elements into a transformed substance. Male and female are the polarities which unite in fusion, and the power, the fire, comes from love and suffering. Gold is produced, but only if there is some 'gold' (aspiration; awareness) to begin with, and the philosopher's stone is the necessary catalyst (perspective; guidance; framework). It was thus for me, eventually, as my life took a new direction.

But that is to jump a little far ahead. For now, some entries continued:

Sunday 2nd February 1975

It is a horrible time to have to make a decision whether to break it off with D. I feel intensely vulnerable, all my resources sabotaged from within. After the events of the past couple of days I feel afraid and humiliated, utterly deeply humiliated. I could still with an effort recover, but should I? Are D's demands on me fulfillable or justified? Will I have to be totally giving and moulding, something I've never yet managed to be? Shall I make this sacrifice?

I am vividly aware of the different roles of man and woman, and of enormous essential differences. This weekend I have felt ashamed of being a woman, ashamed of wordlessness, of the collapse of thought and conceptual ability in the presence of more elemental emotions. Shamed by the time-worn betrayal of the body. I have now only a confused memory of pain and vulnerability, a soft target like a shellfish without its shell! And very alone. I can never look to D for comfort.

"Either sex alone is half itself".

Thursday 6th February 1975

Sheer fatigue has driven me to bed at 8.30, and I have hopes of a solid sleep until the clocks signal the attack of day. "Sounds like a battlefield", a sleepy D, as clocks shot off all over the room this morning.

Perhaps this fatigue induces weakness, but I feel a bone-settling depression, not sharp unhappiness at specific issues, but a hopelessness. I'm not really happy in this job. Often as I sit in the staff-room, nice as it is, I compare with Uni High *(my first teaching job in Australia)*, and visions of sunlight, warmth and lively interesting people float into my memory with a pang of nostalgia. By contrast, this school is like a milk-churn.

Again, rootlessness overwhelms me. I long for stability, to have a focus, a home and the possibility of 'building up'. The old nesting instinct! It is so wearying and non-creative not to be capable of long-term growing: into friends, family, home. I'm getting too old to live in tents!

Monday 10th February 1975

A phone-call from D tells me he will be around later. Deep suspicion! I want to write this out because I am so torn by conflict, and his behaviour is no less contradictory than I suppose mine is, so I suppose we are both torn by the same conflict.

Too unfortunately alike in our less-endearing characteristics, D and I are capable of intense irritation with each other. Gone is the gentle devotedness of the early days.

At present I cannot see why he bothers to walk up the Woodstock Road in a fog.

What does he want of me? What do I give him? I feel that at present I have nothing to give, that my richness is exhausted, if it ever existed. But once I felt it did. D has sucked it out. All I had is eclipsed, and my female qualities challenged and found wanting.

Perhaps it will pass. But at present I have used up all my resources, and found no time to renew them by inwardness. That way lies exhaustion, depression and insanity!

Fear is the bogey, the lurking ghost in the machine, even fear of self, of unworthiness etc. It's as toxic as carbon dioxide to the spirit. Now alone, I am drawing strength from music.

I recall D's words to me early in the relationship, as he tenderly held my face in his hands. "You are so young, and beautiful and full of life. I'm not the man for you.". He was a few years older, which is a lot when you are 25, and don't have equivalent life-experience. These words rang like a knell of prescience long before there were any signs of trouble. He was, however, correct.

He also warned me: "Don't ever lose your freedom." Ironically, it was precisely freedom which I lost, becoming clingy and fearful and unable to function freely as myself. My words in the diary are brave but not percipient, for in emotional states, self-analysis is rarely useful insight into anything, and over these months there was an excess of emotional self-analysis and fluctuations.

Contrary to the impression I convey in some of these entries, D was not a domineering man, simply strong, focussed, insightful and much more mature than I was. Highly intelligent and self-motivated, he did not demand anything of me except to be free and to be myself. It was a combination of circumstance and my own youth which led to my breakdown and collapse of confidence and self-image, hence my sense of having failed us both. However, in hindsight it was an essential proving-ground for the spirit.

Sunday 2nd March 1975

How much has happened this week. It seems many years since the nightmare of the last weeks. It is over. Hard to believe life changes so fast. Now, a sort of reborn person, I look to the future. I am leaving school at the end of term. I know this is right. It is not what I should be doing right now.

Between D and me, the love has come back. Different. Now I trust him. He sent me to the brink, but stayed with me when my own self-esteem was lower than his for me. Only now do I realize the state I have been in these last weeks—all systems completely short-circuited. I feel a bond with him quite amazing to me. At any time, we could decide to part, he and I. I now feel quite free, which is as it should be. Yet in the present I am totally at one with him and feel the unfamiliar sensations of a particular sort of love.

I have always been so sure of equality, of my independence of mind an action. Must I learn that strength wisdom and power for women does not manifest itself in asserting will and demanding response in the same way it seems to do for a man? We are capable of another kind of expression.

I see my Mum with new eyes. Not entirely a puppet of male egotism, she realized and built something strong in her life. In her particular conditions, with the man with whom she chose to make her life, there was only one creative way. Any other would have led to conflict, poverty and emptiness. True submission, or rather *acceptance* (submission to what?) can be a highly intelligent activity, the gift of a proud spirit. I feel myself becoming imbued with her image. My hands are her hands; I see them when I look down, though we are somewhat different personalities.

This may be so, but I'm not sure about my analysis. My mother was sweet and gracious, quiet to the end, with an inner strength rarely seen in action. Wooed by my more assertive father, she complied with his wishes, but I often wondered what talents she may have had which never found expression.

But then, does it matter? They had a good life, with some tragedy, but a life together which was dignified and happy in the way of those born early in the twentieth century, who lived through two world wars, and never indulged in self-importance. She outlived him by some years, declining gracefully, lost in her own thoughts until the age of 95.

Sunday 9th March 1975

Dripping Sunday. No point in getting dressed until ready to face the water, so I will remain in my cell piled high with books. With prices about to double, I feel impelled to stock up. Unfortunately, here there's nowhere to put them; the floor gathers dust in inches each day.

It will be a slow week, but gives me time to read and think. D goes to Moscow tomorrow. A decisive trip I suspect. And decisive for me, to do some thinking.

For me he is no ordinary man, and he was drawn to me as no ordinary woman, both capable of recognising greatness in the other. We were perceiving and responding to something real. What happened?

D recognised the intangibles, but I had to live up to them, and I did not know how. In me they were like a secret horde; talents buried in a field: sterile, useless, unreachable, never deployed. Why did it have to be D, if it leads to awakening by precipitating an end? What if I can become beautiful....?

Not a doing, but a being. I must be free in everything, not seeing slights, not being afraid of a wounding of ego. I can resolve that this is the way it will be. If it is rejected, I will go on loving. And living of course. Without him. It will be a mountainous road, but isn't it what I resolved to follow—not a gentle buttercup path through the plains, but the way through the mountains?

<u>Later</u>

A telephone call before leaving. Nothing could make this week easier to bear. So difficult to believe he still has respect for me, but foolish—he sees too much, too deeply.

I go to bed happy!

CHAPTER 8
Refiner's Fire

———

*T**uesday 25th March 1975***

Tomorrow with the end of school is the end of this phase and a new beginning.

I am probing constantly the nature of Love as if through a dark mist. One cannot catch its outlines; it is now this, now that. Its shape is the shape of living, not some abstract concept. Freely given and taken, without obligation, if it is truly love rather than self-enhancement.

The obligation of love is the commitment to give it the shape and contract needed to sustain it, but without these obligations, one is free. So, it looks like now I am free, despite what I thought and said before. Those were partial grasping in the mist.

Saw King Lear with Michael Hordern. Superb. Lear's curse of Goneril pierced me sharply. I shrank and shrivelled with the horror of it. But this too will pass.

I must break free from my mind. Why am I so enmeshed in thought? I will leave the future free, and start being a lily of the field.

Wednesday 26th March 1975

Miserable again. It's such an old story these days. I wonder if it will ever end. Every meeting with D opens it wider and now there is such nameless pain that I don't know how to deal with it.

I feel such impotence and totally alone. I keep striking walls wherever I turn my heart and mind. Pain is shot with hope; love with despair; liking with distaste; and incomprehension with pain and pain. If smashing my head against a wall would solve anything, I would do it. I think I shall go mad. And my heart and mind will burst. And time itself is a heavy burden strung around my body.

Easter Saturday 29th March 1975

The more I realize how completely and deeply I do and can love, the freer I become. But hardest of all is not to be able to communicate my positive steps to D. I went round for tea. We sat and wrote in almost total silence. He is worried and depressed and I could do nothing.

What I saw in the beginning is the way it should be. The bitterest of all knowledge, that one has destroyed something of the finest, gnaws at my entrails like the fiercest worm.

I came across in William James *(psychologist and philosopher of religion)* something about "man's need to be consoled in his powerlessness, to feel the spirit of the universe recognizes and secures us...". Also, how "religion comes to our rescue...a state of mind known to religious men and no others..."

With all the wish and sympathy in the world, this rings as false to me right now as a cracked gong. I do not expect succour from the "spirit of the universe"! I move with the spirit of life when I am prepared to shoulder my own burdens and continue the struggle in every minute for Truth or whatever. It is such temptation to drop it and cast myself on the "flood and waterspouts of God." What relief it would bring!

I feel that for me this would be wrong, a final act of cowardice, taking the buttercup path. What a paradox though! How can it be both good and yet wrong? I could betray all the power and beauty which my nature can apprehend for something which I'm *told* is 'Truth'. How to know what is Truth?

I was a long way down in the circles of Hell! But I was consistent in my desire to know, and not simply 'believe'. Engaging with doubt is part of the process.

Thursday 3rd April 1975

Where is beauty? I have lost it.

I must lull myself with words and music, other people's beauty. Even the beauty of their pain. Mine is not beautiful. It is ugly I am prey to spectres from the underworld of the unconscious, and feel a gnashing of teeth very close to my heel. I don't know where to turn. Everywhere is a dance of death. I should be on a heath in a storm— a walking ghost.

Sunday 6th April 1975

Well, it's over, the relationship with D. Nothing is to be built. In my view, D and I belong together. I have tried very hard since my collapse putting up with things—too meekly perhaps—but I didn't have the confidence to do otherwise, and I was determined to do all I could to save what should be saved.

I have loved him. I can do no more now. I will live again to find beauty.

From Katherine Mansfield's journal:

"Everything in life that we really accept undergoes a change. So suffering must become Love. This is the mystery. This is what I must do. I must pass from personal love to greater love. I must give to the whole of life what I gave to one."

And CS Lewis:

The surgeon, " if he had yielded to your entreaties, if he stopped before the operation was complete, all the pain up to that point would have been useless".

It is consoling to speculate that there might be a reason and usefulness behind a seemingly bottomless sequence of suffering. That it might be like a journey through the centre of the earth and out the other side—a continuous down-going.

Friday 11th April 1975

This evening, I went to Port Meadow and it was beautiful beyond belief, misty and still, the long twilight of an approaching summer.

Against the supernatural stillness moved the animals: cows, the lithe rhythm of horses across the green, two shy moor-hens busy under the roots and branches of a stagnant pool. And on the flooded meadow, swans feeding intently with sucking noises and the constant curl of probing necks. I watched them for a long time. I can never now see swans in a natural setting without seeing the wintry lake at Coole Park with its spindly trees and the memory of poetry and Yeats.

Also ducks, and one duck accompanied by nine tiny shapes who wheeled and fell out, lined up and scattered until I laughed from the tight knot of pain they evoked in me. That duck and the ducklings were so beautifully in accord with the evening and the rhythm of natural life. Perfection. I felt the dull agony begin again.

No going back—in life or love. No atonement since every act is final and its consequences as irrevocable as ripples and circles in a pool. There is only going on, and new acts of beauty and strength which create their own consequences.

The ebb and flow of tormented thoughts and emotions continued in my diary for another four months until the end of August, when I started to emerge from the darkness with a change of direction. The anguished wrestling does not make good reading, but served a useful purpose, and kept me in the land of the living, able to feel I was processing and transmuting by expressing through words. It was an attempt, via articulation, to stay afloat in powerful seas of emotional currents, which is a metaphor so apt as to be a universal symbolism. Anyone can attest that emotions 'flow' just like water, and their shifting currents carry one's sense of self in all directions, helplessly buffeting the ego in the process. What is needed, ultimately, is a stable foundation of a different order. To begin this work, I took something from the Noah strategy of building an Ark, identifying and holding on to essentials, and waiting for the flood to pass and dry land appear.

Self-pity is not in itself productive, but it can be part of re-balancing if a positive effort is maintained alongside. Sometimes others (friends, counsellors) hold the positive pole for a suffering person so they don't sink. In my case, writing did this, like clinging to a rope to avoid drowning, or onto a flimsy raft on the surges. Later I understood how to build a proper Ark, and the real work on it began in subsequent months.

To sustain the narrative, I will reproduce only a few more representative selections of the entries of this period. The pattern of hard-won glimmers of light oscillating with total despair for long periods will undoubtedly be familiar to anyone who has gone through similar, from whatever cause. The struggle is a human legacy and potential training ground for the spirit.

Sunday 13 April 1975

How to express without triteness the new, ever unique flower of suffering?

Everything is very sharp this morning—the light on my crumpled blanket, the still and silent unconcern of inanimate objects standing where they were put. No breezes from me will move them; just my hand. But the hand cannot deal with the spirit.

To live without hope of dying must surely be the worst one can endure? When even that one sure fact, that one certainty recedes into the void of distant stars?

The final straw is the knowledge that one can bear it, *must* bear it for others who cannot. If I were to give up, take that which should be my right to take—my life—it would not be an act pertaining to myself only. It would be a Symbol, a vast act whose ripples would spread to places I cannot envisage, a force of darkness, fostering ignorance.

Death is a powerful force for the living, and always a Symbol—a controlling and potent symbol. Any death which is deliberate works one of two effects: either of light or darkness. The former, those who accept death for a conscious purpose, stand proud: like Christ, heroes, martyrs, soldiers. But the latter, the suicides, sink heavily into the fabric of the lives of everyone around, and generate more suffering, misinterpretation, despair, nihilism....

I thought my life was my own; it is not. Oh, infinite woe!

This was a significant moment of realization. You never forget moments when genuine knowledge, not just thinking, seems to break through with total clarity, and the surroundings are imprinted in memory along with the realization. I continued for several months more to dwell upon the "midnight with no pain", and encountered it again later in life, but what I knew that morning was inviolable insight.

I see myself sitting miserably with a cup of coffee in a dusty empty room from which a flat-mate had just moved out, contemplating despair and an end to it all. But I also glimpsed the reverberations from such an act of darkness with true horror. With clang like a bolt slipping home was the realization that I had no rights whatsoever over death. Even my own death.

I did not know the beginning, the end, the scope nor the meaning of anything.

LUCY OLIVER

Knowing nothing was my salvation.

Monday 14th April 1975

I must write, if I tear it to ribbons after, without regard for the form of the words, without even allowing the words to form a screen of objectivity, just write the desperate confusion of my thoughts, and if I face everything, perhaps they will resolve themselves into a dew and some clear conviction emerge.....

How is it possible to love so much without burning up?

Am I an awful fool?

Always before I have felt that suffering could be worthwhile in itself; that it would become the fabric of experience; that I would move on.

Am I remembering the first beautiful days when my heart was warm all day with the knowledge that when I returned from school he would be there? When he came and kissed me, and his eyes and hands were full of gifts? How could I have squandered it?

Tuesday 15th April 1975

I cannot bear the grey light of dawn behind the curtains.

Lying on this bed watching the dirty floral through sleepless eyes, and the room takes on that remembered gloom; such beauty, such pain.

Scalding thoughts. Can I exorcise them, these spectres marching with their clanking chains through my mind and heart?

I hear again words: "Come with me to Russia. Come to America—you will have to show her yourself! Perhaps someday, you, wife and mother. We could have such beautiful children. So rich being with you. But I *love* you!"

And I replied nothing, I didn't want to assent so they would stand as stone reproaches if they were no longer meant. I left them hanging there; perhaps he will forget he has said them. Perhaps now, he has forgotten. Would it have been better if I had said: yes, yes, yes with the voice of my heart? Would that have made them true, and sink into the realms of accomplished fact, and not hang before me now like Macbeth's dagger?

How can I carry such memories and go on living? I wasn't worried by the less good times. I expected it to endure. But it didn't. I still cannot believe it.

Tuesday 21 April 1975

An unfamiliar optimism sets in! At last I am here in my new room where I can walk! Birdsongs and sunlight blow in the open window and the room is warm and golden. I like it so much, though the atmosphere is familiar—a sort of quiet afternoon serene room. Gone is that little shoebox of a room with its bitter charge of memories. I always felt caged.

Now it seems like a new beginning. And if I keep careful control against any backward-looking, stop rueing, stop sentimentalizing, stop feeling lonely and aching for love and intimacy, stop the longing....

It could have been, but it is not, and that is an end.

I must think myself into a new pattern.

Oh Death—this beautiful afternoon—the joyous sun—and death would be a gift.....

Sunday 27th April 1975

My thoughts turn often towards death, to that "undiscovered country". I think of "ceasing upon midnights without pain" and of sleep and sleep. But always the knowledge that even then "what dreams may come", as Hamlet was so right to fear.

Is it any more courageous to seek distraction?

I thought I would be wiser by suffering, but what if pain is just wanton and meaningless? And eternal. No necessary end. Once in the swing of it one becomes an initiate, an acolyte. Can I face such a life?

Is it worth it to find that the experience of life was its own 'reward' and one has just got through? To find that the refiner's fire is a limited truth?

Friday 2nd May 1975

Bindings are dropping off my eyes, but slowly and very painfully.

"But that Birth

Was hard and bitter agony for us, like Death, our death." *(T S Eliot)*

What are all the things I have written? They are rubbish.

Wednesday 7th May 1975

These last days suddenly all has changed. My head has stopped spinning, beating frantically through all the darkness, and streaks of light begin to grow.

Oh D, I was not worthy of the love you offered me. The channels in me were not deep enough for its flowing. Now they are deeper, but enough?

I see him anew. Have I thrown away the greatest thing I will ever know? Just as my eyes are opened, it is gone. The very heart of loss.

Tuesday 8th May 1975

Last night I lay in bed, open and vibrant, and examined ways of dying as one compares soap-powders in a supermarket. It is not easy to die—considerately.

I compared gas-oven with poison, with rifle, with cliffs and buses and the sea, and realized that the whole enterprise will require the utmost care and planning! It's simpler to stay alive! It is funny! All the most profound experiences are funny!

But I wasn't chuckling last night because I had a preview of the full awfulness of what I might have to face. Die for it...

Yet I know—oh the wickedness of knowledge! What a cop-out, what cowardly act! When most intense it seems the only end I can bear. But I must bear more.

Must I bear more? Yes. A universal shriek—Yes!

Ah well. It is only weakness. I will keep it in a drawer like a magic philtre, a consolation. If I have recourse to it, I will take the consequences of a weak and paltry spirit.

There are birds singing! Music in their throats joins with Bach through the open windows, and with ripples of sunlight. I don't take them personally any more. They are what I bring to them. Sunlight is just sunlight, and the birds are just another miracle in the crazy miracle of the world.

Monday 26th May 1975

I've been walking with D in Port Meadow in warm blustering sunlight, looking at rippling hillocks of buttercups and daisies. This is England at its best, in sun and summer, lilac in the gardens, meadow-sweet in the fields.

I walked back alone by the canal, loving the leaves and the water and the myriad forms of the back gardens which run down to the water's edge. They were all full of people, weeding, clipping, basking, a sort of halcyon 'summer-ness'. I liked the settled quality of the gardens and occupants because, of course, of the contrast with my life. And turning over the future, the very immediate steps to be taken.

Wanting to leave England and a lust for foreign places. Wondering where to go. Wondering at the fluxes of emotion and of personality. I keep seeing new D's, some of them vulnerable, awkward, non-commanding, and I wonder how much of him is what, and whether I love them all, and whether some are a mask for others....

We continued to see each other from time to time until he left Oxford, but it was torture for me, because all had changed, and continuing in relationship simply prolonged the self-searching and pain, like the lengthy extraction of a tooth with very deep roots.

Sunday 15th June 1975

There really do seem to be people who have the seeds of death flourishing from the start and growing along with them; the people of joy perhaps, because those that are brightest have the darkest shadows.

I saw myself tonight: an intimate stranger, and a woman. This I am. A woman is a collection of forces, but always at one with her body. It is no help to look at men, read their literature, the chronicle of their creation and victories over time, space and themselves, and then feel wanting.

Monday 23rd June 1975

It is worth writing to spread out my peaceful frame of mind on an evening alone in the dusk of my room, in the great double bed, while contemplating a world so unreal and alien to my experience as Russia at the turn of the century. It is difficult even imaginatively to grasp the feverish, tormented quality of those lives lived in poverty, bloodshed and despair, heightened by violence and hope. Such was the relationship of Nadya and Osip Mandelstam in **Hope Abandoned**. (*The author, Nadezhda, was the wife of great Russian Jewish poet Osip Mandelstam who died in a Soviet Labour camp in 1938.*)

"It was then that I first came to know that love is not merely a source of joy or a game, but part of the ceaseless tragedy of life, both its eternal curse and the overwhelming force that gives it meaning." (N. Mandelstam)

I'm thinking that maturity, far from being reached when the flux of adolescence has settled, barely starts until long into adulthood, and probably only gets underway after the age of 50!

Hmm. I wasn't entirely wrong!

Whatever happens in the future, there are moments I want to remember: waking in the mornings, opening one's eyes immediately into the eyes one loves, the first sleepy smile and rolling together. Every morning it is so new and lovely. But these tiny joys soon be over....

Thursday 26th June 1975

It is intolerable! Oh, my heart, crack! Break. Is the spirit indestructible? .....

I have known love too soon. I'm not strong enough, not alive enough within, so that when the case is cracked, the living cotyledon, the germ of life from love, can be vivified. I am a dry land, a barren woman where there are no streams of living water.

I must give him up. It is the only way.

It is Abraham and Isaac. Unless I am able to choose the greater love, love dies.

The simple truth of Calvary.

The language of faith—only these potent symbols have real meaning in extremis. To deny or neglect faith symbols is to shut the gates into the Garden, to turn away from the fountains of living water, hearing only the sounds in the night from the dusty plains of rejection. What hubris it is, really!

Friday 27th June 1975

Particularly enjoyable day punting up-river in S's punt. D and I accompanied him from Osney Lock, which was bright with roses, then up the green river to the end of Port Meadow, while lazing on cushions. We lunched on warm pasties while moored to a windbreak of wild iris by Bossom's boatyard, and the sun glinted over the water.

D and I walked back over the broad windy spaces of the meadow, among the horses and birds, and larks singing on the wing. D is beautiful with animals. He nuzzles the smooth faces and necks of the horses, murmuring gentle loving words. That chestnut foal, so soft and heartbreakingly beautiful.

Sunday 6th July 1975

I can no longer write this journal. I try to write the strong, positive and perceptive thoughts I have, and out comes this drivel! My most cogent thinking remains unexpressed, and always changing, with perceptions constantly altering from one moment to the next, from one suffering to another, from one irritation to the next. Constant change, constant flux. Why? Where is stability?

However, I do have an image of the wisest and most beautiful women I have known or known about; those who have endured the worst and yet are beautiful; those who are helpful to lesser creatures still clambering in the mire. Somehow, this is what I must aspire to.

The hand of an artist can turn pain into a vision of greater truths, so let me look closer at the particular torment which stakes me out on a cross—ah, this is too deep to utter....

My handwriting here disintegrates into a black scrawl and line which runs off the page.

But the next entry marks a turning point. I moved myself and possessions to a new room closer to the centre of town, and the shift of location instigated a new phase in which I gradually crawled out of the circular agonizing and self-flagellation of the previous months. The direction was both inner and outer: on the one hand meeting someone who opened the way to more serious study of the principles and practices which develop the soul, and simultaneously I took up post-graduate study at the university.

The new phase began with a little card with a phone number I had been given by a stranger met at a recent party, and took root in the ancient circle of stones just outside Oxford known as the Rollright Stones.

CHAPTER 9
Chrysalis and Emergence

———

M*onday 7th July 1975*

Saved by Standing Stones!

It was really healing at the last gasp. Such an overwhelming fear and panic gripped me today. Moving house—long hours waiting in the packed-up flat with its load of bitter memories, transportation to a room suddenly alien, too near D—all engendering a sense of utter aloneness and rootlessness. A desperate consultation of the I Ching told me just what I expected and didn't want to hear.

Then I played the card I'd been saving for such a crisis, and went to see a man who is at least in touch with the sort of forces I have been so aware of recently. We drove out through the summer evening of ripening fields and dark clusters of trees and houses, and pubs like hives for all the cars gathered around them, and reached Rollright and the Standing Stones.

The King stone, an enormous impression! So beautiful they all were, each stone an entity, and the whole pattern raised by hands so very long ago. H chanted a haunting prayer as I sat in the centre of the force-field, and all sounds were intensified so that the wind in the grasses rushed like a sea, and an evening bird rang like a bell.

I counted them and came up with the correct number. Congratulated, even this little thing gave me a spark of confidence.

I have learned a lot here, something strange, indefinable. What things, apart from the almost inexpressible sensation from the Stones have I acquired?

I must not give in. I must recover the confidence in my judgement and perception. I must look to the future and be prepared just to wait out the present.

This is all I can do. But I Must Not Give In.

This entry marks a significant shift in my process of coming to terms with volatile emotions. Looking back, I would say, by way of objective analysis, that the moment of choosing to 'play the card', was like flipping a switch to launch a new energy mode.

Then visiting the stone circle earthed it both psychologically and symbolically, because it was very much a departure from my usual awareness, and the whole sequence had an unfamiliarity and new quality.

Wednesday 9th July 1975

How difficult it is! Every day is a struggle, like finding one's way through a blackberry thicket, just going on, continually scratched and torn and yet knowing that one is taking the only course by going right through the middle.

It is the learning of restraint, patience and wisdom, and controlling of the whole quivering animal. It seems very foreign to the way I have heretofore lived. Then I just *was*, and things happened to me! I could have gone on that way, but now I can't.

Self-discipline I realize, is not an arbitrary imposition to exercise the will. This has been my confusion. Nor is it a brake on spontaneity. It is a channel to harness the flow of energies so none are wasted or mis-directed, or spread wildly in all directions, but rather constrained by the guidance of clear vision.

Clear vision? There's an excavation job!

I'm not sure whether realizing the importance of 'self-discipline' was spontaneous, or whether it was influenced by my spiritual, esoteric reading, because I had just started down that path of understanding. However, it was a real insight to finally cotton on to the fact that the raw energy of emotion can be power, if it is channelled and transformed the right way.

My diary over the coming months makes few references to my background explorations into the metaphysical, but it was a time when I began to make connections and to read and think with more purpose and direction. Even though my emotions still continued to fluctuate, I began to think 'outside myself' and to seek a foundation in greater objectivity, which is the beginning of equilibrium between thinking, emotion and action. It begins to shape the soul.

Wednesday 16th July 1975

I feel I should keep the records going. But how to say that I feel I have come to my first birth? That painfully, slowly, light has come back into my life and a small limping understanding—

I have tried to nurture indifference, but that will not do.

So, I will allow love, without reason or bound, and I will wait.

I can wait. My gaze has stilled. I have located the source of love and nothing else has meaning or power to draw me. There is a stirring of a consciousness that I may have work to do, that I have taken the first steps on a long road which will explain many things.

But I am afraid.

Sunday July 20th 1975

I know there are many long dark months to come in which nothing will resolve itself and I will be held fast—like Ariel in the cloven pine. I would like to be absorbed into a whirl of outside activity, travel and projects to make the time go faster, but I think that will not happen.

In one sense it may be a creative period and the foundation of any future work, perhaps the most vital time of my life—if I can not only endure, but maintain the vicissitudes of struggle. The mechanisms of control and creation are at present total mysteries to me. If I am ever to really be capable of love, it will only be then.

At the moment I am still very much a chrysalis struggling in chaos for transformation.

Monday 21st July 1975

I like this bed in my Wellington Square room. A horse-hair mattress on the floor, it is broad and firm and entirely my own, which suits my mood. It is shared only by my efforts at understanding and acceptance. In fact, this room is good. No associations; a temple in the centre of Oxford where I pursue my readings, thinking and language learnings. I'm waiting to hear where in Europe I can remove myself to.

D, though just across the road, I shall not see much more before he or I leave Oxford. Last week I went to his room regularly to watch the Apollo-Soyez launchings and docking in space. Despite execrable television coverage, I was moved by it. However, the enormous distance between D and I now was worse than indifferent, more like a negative force, and made it a painful strain just to sit in silence in the room. I sat there each time in a bottomless well...No I can't write of it. It is still too much.

Friday 25th July 1975

Everything I learn and build up seems to regularly evaporate and I'm right at the bottom again. Perhaps not quite at the bottom—I can see a lapse as just that, a falling-off. Then I feel a power buoying me up, and it seems the help is unfailing when I call for it.

Lord, help thou mine unbelief! How remarkable it is!

Rilke is helping now to take truths into my *substance*, as knowing intellectually is no knowing at all. First build ego structures, and then empty them, so as to be interpenetrated by a finer substance. That's the theory. Human evolution shapes towards the Unity in which the natural world already has its being. Lucky tree and rock, bird and flower—already fully existing without ever having to struggle for it!!!!

I detect the influence of Teilhard de Chardin in my thinking at this point.

Each individual is responsible to the whole of creation for the use he makes of his life.

And D, you who have hurled me into this furnace of truths, and exposed me to love fiercer than I could have imagined, will you be here when I emerge from the furnace? I guess not.

"Sacrifice is nothing but the unbounded, at no point any longer limitable commitment of a man to his purest inner potentiality." *(Rilke)*

Tuesday 29*th* July 1975

This long wait and inaction are becoming very difficult. Even the present moment seems to happen a long way off.

I read, walk and sit in the Parks, and time passes. It is a good moment when I can reach off the light and await the first drills of day in unconsciousness. It is very noisy here. In the hot sun this morning the grinding of machines on the building site had the encompassing relentlessness of cicadas, without their pleasant overtones.

Thursday 31*st* July 1975

I think it will rain. Interesting after a week of hot sunny weather.

Daily something is solidifying. I am conscious of following closely in D's footsteps, not at all my intention, but unavoidable—he's always been there before me!

But the internal gymnastics!

I try so hard to keep measured, and I feel the 'wisdom of the ages' like a tiny grey bud waiting for dedication. I analyse and control, all of which is good and necessary...

BUT

...I'm also raging, and I lie down with death and rise up with Christ, and I swathe myself like a vestal virgin and then cast them off like Magdalene; one minute I bare my breast to the Teeth, and next like Joan of Arc I'm armed to the teeth.

There's no law and no sense in this.

Is Wisdom, at least, a constant?

Tuesday 12th August 1975

Still here!! I seem to be awaiting a summons to go or stay.

I have been walking in the Parks this warm evening, and thinking about the sharp savour living has now—of something no longer taken for granted but having to be struggled with and maintained.

I feel that these weeks are the foundation of the rest of my life. I am entirely alone, and yet 'accompanied'. It is like walking with a pack of dogs; every so often one or all start biting and turn vicious; at other times they are quiescent, snuffling about their own affairs, but always there. A real sense of 'presences', external to me, yet intimately related.

Knowledge, of the sort I seek, is a point beyond which one cannot trace the chain of rationality; a final jump from the nerve-ends which is mysterious and other. But it is no comfort. More like a goad.

Saturday 16th August 1975

Saturday16th August 1975

Perhaps what I feel so strongly is not love, but just desire and clinging. It's an overwhelming *feeling*, but is it true?

Is it like this long-legged fly I see outside my window? He is constantly, persistently thrusting against the glass, determined that there is no glassy illusion and he *will* come in!

I have opened the window a little. He has flown past it, and returned to the illusion. He likes the illusion!

So deeply and completely my heart moves sometimes. It feels so like love. But what if it's an illusion?

(He has come in—the fly!!)

Wednesday 27th August 1975

Yesterday was a very important day, a new chapter I feel.

I went down to London with H to meet the author of the books which have opened doors for me recently.

(This was indeed a meeting of great significance, and the beginning of a long involvement with the western philosophy of the Kabbalah, triggered by the books of Warren Kenton (Zev Ben Shimon Halevi).

I spent the afternoon in the British Museum with the illuminated manuscripts and the Egyptian section. There I was totally absorbed as the sun fell through the windows, a sun of old Egypt, on the silent forms of her living past. The contrast between the silence and stillness of the museum and the teeming forces emanating from stone—the sun seemed to make them dance, like myriad manifestations of the forces of knowledge, emotion, divinity. That great broken head, high, white and all-knowing with the light of the sun.

H tells me there are very powerful and dangerous forces in Egyptology. I well believe it. Those hippopotamus and ram-headed gods were radiating power, a dark power it seemed, a terrible force of attraction. What sort of woman would turn to Taweret at the birth of her child and enlist its aid, I wondered?

From there to Holland Park, and the meeting with a 'whole' man, Warren is sage and prophet of a highly active and contemporary kind. At last, a very ancient wisdom expressed in the twentieth century way of life. He saw round me, and through me and beyond me, and made me see it too. There is a tiny bud in me now, which may enable or force me to go on. It is as if a small hole has been cleared in the clouds of ignorance, fear and aloneness in which I have lived. To know there exists a body of people transmitting the divine in a form I understand! A *body*: a body gives support, caring and structure, and give a single cell purpose, a place, and a means thereby of functioning within a greater whole.

In that room where the afternoon and night moved gently from the garden among the books and symbols, he drew a map of Me from the great cosmos of stars. It was hard but beautiful.

What he said I keep in my heart. It must be fulfilled in action, not words.

Monday September 1st 1975

At a turning point. A lot of new doors have opened. There is the possibility of studying at Oxford, of staying here, of going to Italy—all to be resolved. I will commit to whatever seems right; but what is it?

D left Oxford today. That room is bare. His presence has left it and me, and the whole experience of how the universe turned on its mighty axis and became manifest in one small room is over. And for me it is over. If he were the mechanism of a great lesson, so be it. We will have no business together ever again, and so be it.

Yet I love him, and this love will be the small fire of the rest of my days. The Great fire is what I must follow.

In response to the prompting of a friend that I had the ability to take up further studies, I applied to the university and found unexpected avenues opening towards a new phase of life as a post-graduate scholar.

Friday 19th September 1975

What a strange path my life has taken, a totally new turning, which in the space of a week has transformed my existence.

I sense a band of intellect developing round my forehead! All the rest of me is a total organism, an emotional, spiritual, cyclic being, but warmer and closer to the earth than what I am going to be this year—a female mind in a college full of females!

The man I have loved returned to Oxford yesterday, briefly, and remains in this country several weeks more. It awoke all that end-of-the-world sense of loss, when bright visions of the future turn to premonitions of exile and life separated from its source. Paradise Lost, which I suppose is enacted sometime in every life.

CHAPTER 10
The Presence of Absence

———

*T*uesday 23ʳᵈ *September 1975*

Today miracles were accomplished because both the Faculty Board and LMH accepted my applications without demur. And I have been offered a basement flat by the College. Amazing!

With everything fallen into place I went on a stroll of exploration through the gardens of the college. The afternoon sun shone calmly on the lawns, and through the trees and long grasses down by the river. I shall love these gardens.

H drove me out this evening to the Abbey at Godstow. There was a very bright full-horned moon, and near it, a brilliantly rayed Venus, hanging above the dark river-trees and broken outline of crumbling walls in cold misty air. I communed with these celestial bodies, and the moon really seemed like a sister—a ruthless, remote, cyclic being.

'And the moon thereof is my body' I thought, and almost prayed that she would take care of my body, as my mind's needs have been amply rewarded by miracles.

Sunday 5ᵗʰ October 1975

Having no place to go in these awkward days between leaving Wellington Square and moving into the new College flat, I betook myself to Paris. My belongings are scattered around Oxford, some kindly taken in by my Pakistani landlord.

Paris was pleasant enough, despite moments of depression in my hotel room by the Gare du Nord. What am I doing here alone in a dingy hotel room, in this city of arrogant people, myself deaf in one ear, temporarily homeless, and missing desperately love lost? Images everywhere of love and I, desiccatingly alone again, tramping the streets looking for shoes.

Montmartre on a warm grey Saturday morning, pushing through crowded streets mutely examining racks of shoes for the mythical shoe which not only appealed, but fitted my large *pied*. It was not to be!

But on the other side of the balance, moments of great joy, like Monteverdi Vespers in St Germain-des-Prés, a pulsing, aethereal version in the great church.

And the Atelier de Brancusi. Here was tranquil perfection. I sat quietly in a corner: light from the roof on the still stone; the gleaming forms of the Neophyte and Leda. It was so beautiful, and filled my soul, and I thought here is God made manifest in the simple forms of essences rendered lovingly by a simple man who had learned how to give form to soul.

Each sculpture on its rough-hewn pedestal was as full as the centre of a rose, and seemed to spill over its completeness into some other dimension. I touched them lovingly. My hands took on the cold sheen of bronze, the rough grain of wood or crumbly concrete.

The Bird soared there, among huge white Coqs. On the floor, the World Egg, and shining in quintessential innocence, the primeval Neophyte. Ah bliss!

But I had to leave there to join the rush of Paris traffic, ceaseless in the sunset by the Seine. It was my last evening. I had stayed an extra day because of meeting Professor S, a one-eared behavioural scientist, who took me to dine with his gentle psychiatrist friend in the Boulevard Beaumarchais. A beautiful apartment, three fine children, perfect mannered and charming; delicious dinner provided by Madame, extra guest notwithstanding. The conversation I had difficulty in following. It was interesting but slightly strained, and further strain followed as I firmly insisted that I was not going to spend the night with Prof!

Now I have finally settled in the flat and turned the room into the same old me. Is it the same old me? The room looks like it. H insists I am not, and that I shall look for different things from life and love.

In fact, these days the old love is becoming somewhat remote, and is becoming more a stranger, not a Beloved lost. Goodbye, once so much beloved! You are becoming a shell in my memory, the fragile shell of a man from whom for me the real vivid essence is gone, receded beyond my knowing or caring.

But as I write, tears are forming. It does not do, yet, to stir a wound so deep.

On Tuesday I went to Swyre Farm (*a Sufi centre*) for the Night of Power, when the angelic world comes to earth. I was apprehensive, but found the zikr beautiful, the movement and chanting. Ibn

Arabi I can embrace. He speaks in a language I can understand and tells me things I do not know. It is good.

And always there is the Tree.

The Tree of Life: my studies into the structuring principles of the Kabbalah which became more and more interesting and formative, and began to give some shape to my emotional turbulence. Gradually I learned perspective, universal laws of inter-relationship and the creative, which in time ordered and transformed the mental, emotional and bodily cauldron of energies into which I had plunged so precipitously.

Thursday October 23rd 1975

I am reluctant to come indoors as without is a day basking in its own beauty. Late Autumn, the trees only just now turning golden, ripening it seems, in the sun.

I have been cycling around on my new bicycle, absorbing the day. I am very contented. Life at last is full and feels right. Last night I became aware that however totally I am absorbed in my work, friends and role here, it is only a half of me really. Yet it is right, for now. I have to cultivate trust, that life know what is best!

I am obsessed with anthropology. My first essay on Malinowski and the Kula ring was fascinating and well received.

Enjoying cycling. Enjoying friendship with S.

Sunday 26th October 1975

Sunday afternoon taping Mozart. The Autumn-ness of this last week has been superb. The leaves are continually falling, it is mild, and for once seems full of promise of good things—cosy room, Mozart and requisite study! Good things!

Though I am swallowing constantly memories of last year. As the days pass, memories of D unfortunately grow not lessen. They are further away, but more beautiful, and I am still bemused by the fact that now, only a year after our meeting, I am alone. And the sadness that may suddenly afflict me at odd moments is not of nostalgia, or even regret. It seems like pure sadness, if such a thing exists

It is all remote. My lost Love, unworthy being, how I miss you!

Not very constructive thoughts. In fact, I am full of positiveness and enthusiasm these days. Ancient sorrows rarely interfere with the purpose of my days, and I am careful to avoid things which may occasion them.

Thursday 30th October 1975

Anniversary of my birth, quarter of a century ago! How strange to be able to talk in centurion terms! Now I've really arrived!!

And today I have been given the gift of peace. The last two days have been a bit rough, crying most of the time—a little unusual. I blamed it on the pills the doctor ordered for my infected ear. But it was deep, whatever it was, missing D. Why did it occur now? He has no place in my life and I had ceased to think of him.

But the anniversary of our meeting looms, and I wrote to him a letter I will never send:

"D, I miss you. More and more as the days pass, I feel your absence intruding on my daily routine, where thoughts of you have no place. It is not thought, but I feel you should be here. In all that is beautiful, as the year turns to the time when we met, I remember you.

Dear Love, I miss you. Our time was so short. After that January day when you knocked the ground out from under my feet, I could never talk to you again. The mere sight of you closed me in a shell all those months. And now I have become whole again, I remember you as first you were, or as I was, and all the dark months have merged to underline the fact that I love you. I fight it, but it is there. There's nothing I want from you, yet I feel you are missing. I don't understand it.

But you are gone, and this is a silent call.

Know this—my love goes with you and always shall, not through will of mine, but because it is so—irrationally, insanely—my love, my lost Love.

D, I miss you so much."

But today was peaceful. I went for a Birthday Walk in the Parks. An incredibly beautiful Autumn, standing by the rushing water, watching the yellow chestnut leaves imaged in the ripples, distorted but beautiful. Image of images. Prayed for clear vision, a vision which is still, and reflects the clear outlines of the leaves, not distorted by any medium of reflection.

Clarity of vision.

So that is the quality of this birthday, and the goal of the next 25 years. It seems to have taken all this time to arrive at the beginning of real development. Here's to acceleration!

Sunday 2nd November 1975

This constant sadness—is it the quality of maturity as opposed to youth? It seems to underlie all things, even the joyful—the sadness of the world as it is, imperfect. A sense of loss, not the depression of youth, springing from self and confusion, but a clear knowledge that things are as they must be, and it involves loss and sorrow.

When I wake in bed at night, and constantly in all perception throughout the day, I have a deep sense that all is not right, but that it is irremediable. However, I do feel for the first time, that it is I who holds the reins of my life and destiny.

I miss D. His absence is like a presence always at my side. I have dismissed it as nostalgia, but it feels less like emotion than a deeper level of knowledge, and as such, it might have come to stay. People do carry a portfolio of ghosts and ancient sorrows.

If now I am conscious of this huge arrow in my back, it is for a purpose. I must learn to live with and through it. Pain is a tool which can be used creatively with fine precision. And one must retain faith that after the waning of the moon, it will wax again.

Work to do!

Thursday 13th November 1975

A Most Final Song

I have just been told that D is living with another woman. This I must face. This man, to whom I have given so much, can I imagine him now with another? It must be done—I pray for strength, that I may be able to see things as they are and must be—Oh D, you whom I have so loved—so soon, so soon and you have another.

I can almost not weep. I am deep, still, and far away in a land where the air is pain and no being moves on the face of the ground—that I may live to learn from this, as it is said—that one is never given greater suffering than one can bear?

My love, you who were loved and brought me to birth, to knowledge, may you find in the arms of another woman (so soon, so soon!) what you failed to find in mine, may you find that eternal complement the poet in you seeks, and the eternal torment sought by the artist. You will find comfort and oblivion, but only you know wherein you will find the ultimate goad—may you find it and do what you must, and not live to dissipate the great gifts you have been given for want of something which you cannot find.

May she love you, my lost and last darling, for in the marble of my memory, that you will always be. You fructifier; may she love you for always as perhaps I could never.

And if this is the last rhapsodic outpouring of love as it dies—oh those swans! —may I live to see sense and what is real. Those swans—how clearly in my dream the two white birds entwined in a humming purple landscape, falling, falling, and as they fell, necks intertwined to their death, that last song, that awful beautiful song, vibrant in the purple reeds—this dream was a message I cannot ignore.

Adios! How many times have I still to face such torment, every time as new as before? It is so strange, is it not, that beauty comes to naught?

I am no longer in any sense his woman. I have gone from him.

There is such silence in this room. I have never known such silence.

Sunday 16th November 1975

Love seems so absolute that the entire universe seems unstable when it fails. I was conscious of a force far beyond me which seemed quite capable of calling a universe into being, creating stars and planets and even the complexity of man.

But what happened? What can suddenly defuse this sense of power into a small pile of grey dust? Seems unanswerable. Of course, I am richer in my experience, but that Me hardly seems reason enough for such large shenanigans.

Anyway, here I am, surprised and better off! Forgive me, Universe, if I say that at the moment, it doesn't quite seem worth the pain. I know I'm being obtuse. And I'm finding it hard to find a substitute for all the music and tapes we listened to together; and the pictures, clothes, odds and ends which bear his imprint; to say nothing of the sight of a winter sky, the gloom once radiant for me with an inner sun.

But I'm calm today. With this last act of writing, all trace of D is eradicated from my life. Not for a single moment shall I entertain the thought of him in any guise.

'The Great man changes like a tiger'. (*I Ching*)

There will be no further mention of D in these pages. I will go forward with joy to what is right.....

CHAPTER 11
Going Forward

———

Saturday 21ˢᵗ November 1975

A great change in the quality of life, and blessed change and relief from Oxford. My head is presently filled with images of brilliant countryside and sunshine.

Last night, suitably decked out in long dark dress and with a very positive frame of mind carefully in place, I thoroughly enjoyed a Strauss evening at LMH, danced, laughed, met people, and it was a real tonic to my jaded expectations of social events. At the end I met J, and went with a group of friends to a pub outside Oxford. Feeling all the fates were very much with me, I then went out to his little Oxfordshire village.

I woke this morning with sunlight through the cottage windows, quiet square sounds of farm vehicles. It seemed heaven on earth for peace and rusticity. J I like very much, and somehow, he seems to fit into my life at this point.

The Cotswolds lay clear and remarkably rich on one of the most perfect days this time of year can offer. Again, I felt the gods were smiling. So many images—I hadn't realized I was so starved for natural beauty.

Then the Hunt came through.

Picture a quiet, nay, supernaturally still and sheerly silent valley, with a small village fitted along it; all hillsides landscaped and ridged, as we watched the drama of the Hunt with gathering emotion (word chosen with care!)

The fox streaked desperately along a wall, across a road beside a wood. We watched and my heart rose into my mouth at the anguished beauty of it. Some distance behind, the hounds followed, white specks fanning across the hillside, 'giving tongue' as they caught the scent.

But there, still, like a waiting army, the hunters gathered on the hillside, red against the ploughed earth. It was like watching a huge ritual battle, for blood was the goal and desperation was balanced against the cold intelligence of man. Strategically, on different hills, the hunters waited, tactics as controlled as a ballet. The horses thundered down the hill as the laws of the chase took them, out from the woods, behind the grey stone village walls.

And my thoughts:–whatever sort of people these are, they have their roles. All have roles, the hunters and the hunted; those rotten with wealth; the always homeless, poor and with but little time to live; and the spectators, those who play all parts and watch the spectacle of life. All are hues of the earth.

Returning from tea at Stow-on-the-Wold, the entire sky took fire. I had asked just for a sunset, not such stupendous prodigality! I have felt blessed and give thanks.

Thursday 4th December 1975

I'll use this afternoon to gather myself up. In the hustle of term's end and new contacts, so easily one goes off the deep end and loses the quality of life in the play of its surfaces.

The sun is low, though only 2.30pm. It is winter; mercifully I have been spared the brunt of its memories and chill. There is too much to do! It is such a different winter from last, thank God. There is J and his cottage and the Cotswold countryside. Lunched at Broughton-on-the-Water yesterday, fine food, wine and chatter, and then back in the car through the glimmering unreal light of sun-set at this time of year on stone cottages, and stick-woods mustered on the crests of dark rolling fields.

But I was thinking: 'ware, 'ware, Lucy!! Do not lose direction. Perhaps because of reading 'The Waste Land' and Scott Fitzgerald, I became aware of a restlessness, and of the emptiness of the spaces in between. Things have arisen as fill-ups I think, to remove the dangers lurking around this time of year. I am grateful. Must not abuse.

Friday 12*th* December 1975

Life continues. Warm spaces move in and out, and are gone again.

As suddenly as it began, my two-week encounter with F ended, and Caribbean warmth went back to its source. 'Just a dream', he said, and it is, already. A presence lingers for a time, then grows cold. I accepted it all, without emotion or deep thought, just a pang of regret that something warm and life-filled, tasting of sunshine and brightness has left the cold foggy days to wreathe their chill over the dead wintry land. All bright things extinguished must be!

Am I learning just to watch things come and go; give and take when there, bid farewell when it must go? Now it is; now it is not, and these are no farther apart than a hair.

So, goodbye Bright one, goodbye Brown one.

Monday 15th December 1975

Wild days! I can't take this pace!

Returned from Cotswolds today with S after an evening's heavy drinking at Chequers with dancing and other drunken activities in the company of J and C! We had lunched at the Rose Tree, and it didn't stop!

Returned through very heavy fog on a chilly day to an Oxford already seeming deserted for Christmas, and feeling a bit disoriented at the thought of the drear days ahead. It will be a particularly empty Christmas, but I must bear up.

Friday 19th December 1975

The siege begins after return from a whirlwind London trip.

Lunch at Hennessy's on Wednesday: long, be-barrelled sombreness draped with Christmas tinsel, and very much an olde-worlde London atmosphere. Ballet of Romeo and Juliet at Covent Garden in the evening. Quite beautiful—images of a tiny Juliet blowing across the stage in a gauzy picture of innocence and beauty. I shed several tears as she mourned alone on a vast empty stage, in silence.

Dinner afterwards in Covent Garden. C and J in good form, jesting furiously. Stayed overnight at C's on Highgate Hill, and awoke just in time to meet S and C in El Vino's, Fleet Street for lunch and champagne. Very journalistic, and even more so at the Sunday Times party we looked in on later. It was full of the intelligent rag-tag and bobtail of a newspaper world. The day ended with oysters and ice-cream, and I returned to S's flat in Hampstead to stay last night.

It seemed like days of driving in London traffic. What a city! As ever I didn't feel enough at home to live there. It is a mecca, a city of ugliness and excitement for me, but I feel I could not live in it. However, I must say I enjoy this expensive frenzy every now and again!

Phoned Mum and Dad this morning, which seemed easier than dialling another London number, where the lines are always clogged. Amazing to hear their voices so easily across 12,000 miles!

Sunday 21st December 1975

On this, the shortest day of the year, the light on this grey afternoon is the light of last year and I wonder again, as so often—will I ever get over it?

<u>Later</u>

Yes, I shall. Walking back from the Common Room late, the night was totally clear and not cold. The nights I can bear; therefore, I must endure the evenings like a bout of nausea. I had my thousand days and escaped with my head. Many women have come out worse. Is there ever suffering so great that a thousand million others have not known and survived? A tiny drop in the ocean, transmuted with that of all others, and great thoughts can be born

168

of it. From the perspective of Tipheret on the Tree, (*centre point of Essence on the Tree of Life*) one can see the threads, and the mechanics are visible for what they are within the beauty of a greater order.

Monday 22nd December 1975

Monday 22nd December 1975

The workings of chance are outrageous! Who should I see loping down Walton Street this afternoon but He Who Shall Not be Named! My eyes turned inside out. I resolved to return to Little Clarendon St where I'd just been talking with our mutual friend, and ask about this apparition, if said friend were still there, and if not still there, to forget the whole thing.

He was still there of course!

Apparently, HWSNBN did get on a plane to leave, but changed his mind. 'She' must have a very powerful attraction! In between cursing the old m-f, I have to laugh; it is so predictable.

But God in heaven, why make me see him? Why must I know exactly where he is always? As soon as he gets further away in my awareness, something new comes to light and I find out.

After this distraction, I continued to my intended destination, (a further ironical quirk,) to Port Meadow. Sat down among the cows. Smoked a cigarette. Port Meadow does not change: those horses, grey trees, mud, light sky. And the wheel had come a full circle.

But not complete. Oh God, not complete. This, my 'Heath' of the greatest moments of my life; its rolling ground, soothing as the motion of a body. I <u>shall not despair</u>.

But the air is so thin. With no possessions, and no clothes or coverings, Poor Tom's a-very cold. And there's this wind, always. All that vibrates does not sing.

And so again I say; 'Goodbye Dearest, Dearest, most Dear.'

This time the last time.

Ah—the agony! The emptiness!

Tuesday 23rd December 1975

It is silent now, late, and only the wind is knocking at my window.

I guess everyone must at some time "stand with the stupid look on his face of a man whose guts have just been kicked out." *(Bogart in Casablanca)*

"And more and more often it happens to me that I can't say 'I am' but that I have to say 'It is…' but then I mostly fall silent." *(Rilke)*

"And as he died

As gently as if without a name,

He was shared out:

His seed ran in brooks,

His seed sang in the trees and looked at him from the flowers.

He lay and sang."

(Rilke, Book of Hours)

DIARIES OF A YOUNG MYSTIC

Wednesday 31st December 1975 11.30pm

Thank God—the last time I shall write this year! I have never seen a year out with more fervour in the metaphorical boot. As S and I wished ourselves joy for the New we consoled ourselves: 'It couldn't possibly be worse!'

I'm glad to be alone and quiet now, in bed, a New Year candle holding out hope in the reaches of the room. What a strange year for me. More than ever before it is a different person at the end; my whole core has changed.

Here's to a quiet life! Consolidation!

God help me!

I am now living in a basement flat near LMH during the mid-winter break between terms.

Tuesday January 6th 1976

Kazantzakis said: "We do not fight our dark passions with a sober, bloodless, neutral virtue which rises above passion, but with other, more violent passions." The words of a great Fighter! I think Kazantzakis was somewhat trapped in poetry, but what a warrior! A a poet of the struggle, but therefore unable to find even limited real freedom. Perhaps this is his greatness—the expression?

I have fallen into a pleasant pattern these days of working and reading. This afternoon I have my window open onto a very still waiting garden, a mild breeze and sound of birdsong. I dread the coming of term and the whirlwind of people and activities it brings.

But being alone and content can't last. Re-fuelling interludes! I have never been gladder to have entered a new year, just for itself and without hope. One feeds off Hope: hope for the realization of this or that dream; hope for the future, hope for happiness. So, perhaps to be truly free to start the journey, Hope too must go.

"Poor Tom kept not a rag". *(King Lear)* Yet, if we are only "such stuff as dreams are made on", then we "will fade and leave not a rack behind". *(The Tempest)*. So, our part in creation must be active, and according to the Kabbalah, we do it through the Beriatic world, which is the creative realm beyond our normal psychology. For Kazantzakis it's a matter of creating God, liberating Him from matter. For Teilhard de Chardin we must create higher and higher life. This struggle for creation has suddenly become very real to me. Although with reservations about the details and language, the sweep of Teilhard's thought has struck bindings off my mind. We may think the Great Galactic Universe is the very least of horizons we should be working with, yet that is still only a vision of matter!

What of my life? My little Lucy-life seems to have evaporated as an entity. There is only a dynamic process, an on-going struggle to liberate the joy in things.

In dynamism lies stillness. In the heart of battle—peace.

But if you clutch at Peace, it slips away, and is a mirage. If the world desires peace, it has a lot more fighting to do! This is a great paradox. There is power in opposites, but one must know when to be active and when to be passive.

Thursday January 8th 1976

Thoughts in the middle of the night. (Why is it only just before my brain gives out entirely, when all is dark and still, that big thoughts `communicate?!)

I am thinking that Art, being a conscious creation, is great, but greater than Art is all that is *not* said in any poem, all that is *not* there in any painting. The movement of the hand that holds the brush is greater than anything actually painted. The action is Life, the ultimate artist.

Rilke's : "...and then I mostly fall silent."

Sunday 11th January 1976

There are changes taking place in me, in this solitude; each day I feel I have travelled a thousand miles. I feel that my mind is formless, like the first matter of creation, and all that enters takes and forms it.

So many things seem to be settling quietly into place—like sand when the turbulence of sea has become calm. I have moments of impatience, and moments of panic. The sooner I take my life on my shoulders, the better, but remembering: not I, but God in me.

My dreams of 'Lucy's life' as I conceived it, are gone. If solitude, solitude it must be; if scholarship, scholarship it must be; if eternal wandering, that it must be. However, it does make life sort of sexless!

Paradoxically, I think the prostration of a Knight before his Lady is actually forceful and potentially dominating.

Tuesday 13th January 1976

How far this month is already gone! I had thought January the longest month—well-nigh eternal! How different this year from last, when indeed it was.

I woke this morning to an early alarm-clock from an exceptionally late night (4am) finishing an essay. The weariness brought it all back, and I again felt a wave of that indescribable deathlike torture of waking all those mornings. By contrast, my life now is ethereally blissful – waking naturally, rising in peace to the always full and simple pleasures of breakfast with a book and a day spent calmly at activities most fulfilling! I resolve never to waste a minute of this pleasant year. But already January is half-gone!

Still, I haven't been guilty of wasting too many minutes in the last couple of weeks. Been very active reading and thinking: Rilke, Teilhard de Chardin, Kabbalah, Charles Williams, Yeats, Book of Kells, Rembrandt, Levi-Strauss and much ethnological reading and thinking about "moral axes on a social graph", dimensions, conflict and women. Also, esoteric stuff on witches and symbols.

I feel quite alert and full of enthusiasm, overwhelmed by how much I want to absorb, and all at once!

This evening I've read half of Malinowski's 'Diary' with great fascination. A genuine specimen of the Late Romantic: hedonistic, sensitive, intelligent, lazy, sentimental and romantic. He *sucks* at the world around; tries to draw it all inside himself, the beauties, atmospheres, even the rottenness – self-conscious anal-ness and enjoyment of distaste. The poetic nostalgia, wistfulness and mist of senses —entirely self-obsessed. He had the temperament of a poet but not the control or objectivity. Baby-like. But I understand too well—I'm not so different myself!

I never recorded some of the dreams I had last year around the traumatic time of August '75– clear powerful messages from the unconscious if ever there were. All are water dreams, and they made a great impression on me at that time of terrible decision. It was reassuring to have guidance, to know I was dealing with forces powerful and conscious enough to make statements through dream, when my thinking was out of action.

In retrospect, those dreams were more significant than I thought at the time. All involving escape or rescue from surging water or the ocean, they embodied the turbulent emotions surging through me, and the rescues involved a calm, potent female figure who warned me of the waters encroaching, or herself entered the water in my place. I knew she was also 'me', but old and knowing. My real identity. When this 'other' emerges, generally due to some shock or crisis, it has real power, and is characterized by a tendency to forget it afterwards as the normal mind and identity reassert themselves.

As well as via dreams, the 'other self' manifested in some real-life incidents, for example the trivial incident I described on April 9th 1974 when I located the stolen paddles on our punting excursion. It was not quite so trivial in retrospect, because it was a real-life manifestation of a powerful change of state, precipitated in that case by sheer indignation. My actions took' normal me' quite by surprise, but the whole incident almost wiped itself from my memory immediately afterwards, until something in me woke up further down the river: 'Hang about...what just happened...?'

The water dreams continued, until with my whole being I had made a renunciation and decision to submit to whatever needed to happen.

Then came the Transformed dream.

It was the same scenario, but this time I was in the waves, being hurled and bounced and thrown about in their arms, and calling in joy from sheer happiness and exuberance. I could swim at last! Fear gone, immersed and joyous in the watery medium.

The only other dream I have had in my life with this sort of clarity and urgency is that dreamed so many years ago in childhood, which found its literal fulfilment last year in the Oxford market when D enacted it, caressing the bright face of a pansy. Perhaps I needed the clinching sanction of a powerful dream to release such currents of powerful emotion. I don't know. It still surprises me, and seems contradicted by events, but the Kabbalah teaches that the exception to a rule is when one moves into a world or level where different rules apply. I must accept that the meaning was not what I had assumed in the old order, ie. that this man was the final culmination of my search.

It has been a glorious winter day today, mild and shining with sun in the Parks, where great uprooted trees lie about like corpses, the air vacant and empty where they had stood. Such gales we get in this small isle! Wish they would blow it further south!

I am starting to feel that the base for the next phase of my life might be here, on this side of the world rather than the other. Well, can't be helped, and who knows what direction things will take?

Wednesday 14th January 1976

I realized cycling to Kabbalah group this evening, under a large silver moon in a mild clear sky, that I could say that I was happy and be so. Once I almost thought I would never be able to say it again, and that struggle would always be a balance between moments of joy vs. slog and trial.

Friday 16th January 1976

I have seen a terrible vision—the loneliness of the Creator as long as his creation exists separate from him, and that of Creation when separate from its creator. Every Creator, and every conscious creation, for are we not all involved in the creative somehow? Our life depends on it.

What made me see this horror was meditating on love and its enormous energy as I felt it move through me with the thought of D. It is the fire which burns life into my days, yet no longer *of* him. It no longer matters that it will never reach him because he has expanded into the world. But it's such a force, still!

Unknowingly, he has been the instrument to breathe life into a puppet (like Pinocchio!), to give me a voice and something to sing about. Even if never again, he has been a Creator. He has gone, but he gave a living gift which will continue to grow, but only in his absence. And that's the way it must be.

So, I still think about the unmentionable it appears! Often and always. His image walks with me (how could love ever cease, and thereby negate its previous existence?) but it is a past image in present reality. Oh D, how can I even speak of it, what is still so real, strong, so pulsating-ly present?

And the real physical you? Where are you? What doing? I shall never know, nor must I.

With the advent of Google, this changed. Somewhat more than twenty years later, I had the idea to do a google search, from curiosity mainly. I knew he had gone to a big country which suited his scale, but he had always intimated that he did not expect a long life. So, it was poignant but good to find him alive and established in a career in the States, and the awareness of him there lingered in the background of my heart for the next ten years.

Recently, I again decided to check. This time I found a very recent obituary, and the world became a little emptier.

I mourn his passing still.

When Rilke wrote of women and angels, did he see the thorn right dead centre? That the woman who wears the rose must also carry the thorn digging into her flesh – at just about the heart, I'd say. Did Rilke see that he himself was greater than his Messengers of Light, for he had a voice to reach from earth to heaven, he was a source and creator, while angels are merely created? The Orphic voice—more articulate and generative than the love of women.

It is true that we create, in the sense of giving form to angels, whose reality lies in those forces and powers which impact on our psyches with an imprint of divinity, a shift beyond normal human.

I played Purcell's Queen Mary's funeral music earlier. Recorded about this time by D, it contains now all the love I knew then, and all the deaths of the following months when I played it so often to help distance the rawness of personal grief in something larger—the death of the Queen, the Great Mother par excellence. It doesn't enter through my ears, but lands straight in my soul by a process of osmosis!

Earth's creation is unbalanced, a one-way outflow only ended when it wraps itself up, back into the Unity, or when a created entity makes that return journey. I think the world's history must be in its merest dribbling infancy!

A practical principle I am recognising, is that when a question is articulated, the answer comes into being in the same instant, (or at least the possibility of it,) for the answer is evoked through the question. Like Life and death, I suppose.

Sunday 18th January 1976

Sunday 18th January 1976

Spent the weekend in the Cotswolds with J. Walks in the vivid countryside; big ricks of sweet-smelling hay; huge dumb bullocks breathing clouds of steam into the straw-spread mud. Very rustic.

We cooked a pheasant on Saturday evening and dined with ceremony beside the fire, with Xmas pudding flambéd in sheets of blue flame.

After an incursion into Haute Couture, suggested by the chestnuts lying in the coals - when he insisted in dressing me from head to foot in silver foil (shining to say the least!)- we shared some original creative works with each other. For the first time I read a couple of my poems to an outside ear, and was greatly encouraged and delighted by his appreciation of them.

Today we spent reading the Sunday papers. In all, a weekend of very congenial pursuits.

New term begins. Must be disciplined.

Saturday 24*th* January 1976

A day for praising!

Woke up and observed another day of brilliant sun and blue sky, so decided to go for a walk. I stepped outside the warm flat into the expected mild air....what a shock! The air was composed of ice!

I hurriedly dived inside and added several layers and scarf, and set off across frozen puddles. Delighted by the frozen duck-pond with the ducks skidding across the surface and going under in splinters of ice. The sun was warm and brilliant, until suddenly from the North, snow started to fall. Ecstasy! I love the transformation wrought by snow, and uttered bubbles of praise to the universe.

Monday 2*nd* February 1976

Candlemas, and truly the world was white aflame today!

Woke up in the Cotswolds and all the village was white. It had been snowing all night. After our usual late and leisurely breakfast, I set off for a walk. How strange snow is!

It was so silent everywhere; no movement, no birds, but the white lane stretching up the hill and all that still countryside. Loved it. It seemed another world, a world where beings ranged abroad, and all the normal order was suspended.

Huge three-pointed footprint of some great bird marching before me down the lane. Must have been a pheasant. Brown and white hill tossed to the skyline. The wood blasted and broken in recent gales was bathed in white, and verily, a unicorn could have been among the magic tangle of brush.

J. joined me and we gathered the white fine powder into snowballs. Driving back to Oxford we got stuck off the road. The wheels spun and we had to go back into a field and make several runs over the ice and frozen grass.

In Oxford I walked back through the Parks. River frozen black with great sweeps of purest white, and bare willows hung against the preternaturally still and transformed river.

Sunday 8th February 1976

Sunday 8th February 1976

A gentle Sunday evening settles. As the last light moved in the west, I felt it came from the Meadow and wanted to be out there with the animals and the water. But duty calls!

Then all the panoply of cloud and light suddenly was driven out by a grey sky mass; now it is darker all at once.

Have read Faust this afternoon. All that gothic spirit in the quiet of my room speaks very loudly! So many things stirring in me these days, it's difficult to devote time to Weber and Durkheim when there are a million and one things to be thought, read and explored.

Somehow, they all fit in; my essays are produced on cue etc.

The serial aspect of time's workings has just got to be accepted!

LUCY OLIVER

Friday 13th February 1976

A letter on the eve of St Valentine.

"Beloved, you will not know my valentine. I will send you a gift of such richness, such love—but you will not know its source.

Perhaps for you it will come as a moment of intensity which will open a pathway to the stars. Or maybe a corner of the veil will fall, briefly, and the knowledge will stay with you always as another turn of the key.

Perhaps it will come in the arms of a woman whom you love or who loves you; perhaps you will meet her as you once met me, turning the corner among the fruit of a Saturday market.

Perhaps there will come a flash of sun which lights the globe from end to end; or gently, through rain on a river.

Howsoever it comes, take it as my gift to you, and as violently pure as the flame of this love and pain in which I have learned to live. So will it be."

Tuesday 17th February 1976

It is extraordinary to explore memories via concentrated recollection. Memories of childhood, for instance, which were not consciously recorded and never knowingly remembered, are yet able to be entered again with total recall of extraneous, insignificant detail.

Last night before sleep a whole flood of perceptions and sensations of myself as a small child became real and present. I have never before even thought about the regular family rite of visiting the cemetery and tending the graves of family departed. But suddenly last night, I perceived this repeated ritual in every detail, and not just on one visit, but in parallel, on many different occasions, as if flipping pages of memory. I was completely there in situ, observing the changing light of different times and occasions, and aware of my internal thoughts and preoccupations in the locations on different occasions and as I grew older. I was also aware of the unchanging, stark beauty of the rite of visitation itself, and the mythical quality of it all, in the role of an observer from the future.

I saw two old people standing before the grave of their son in silent remembrance; a small child (myself) is playing among the graves looking for white doves in the glass memorials. Everywhere sun, cypresses and peace. How well I remember every detail, how vividly, how cumulatively precise!

What is this facility of *detailed embodied memory*? I note that time worked differently as a child. Our walk down the entrance road lined by cypresses up to the cemetery gate seemed to go on forever, as if time had got stuck somewhere in the middle of the walk. My child's world was self-enclosed, with only vivid points retained in memory, but when I sink in deeply now to excavate the situation, I find that absolutely *everything* is recorded, every minute detail not even noticed at the time.

Every mark on a wall, every shift of the light, every leaf on a bush can be dredged from the depths of a memory which has no location.

Where are these memories stored? So intact, so sensory, undisturbed and seemingly non-existent until a probing conscious light is directed into the archives? Weird!

Saturday 6th March 1976

Materiality is very frustrating! I was all morning wrestling with my 'mineral friend', my cycle, but right at the end I cannot re-fasten the nuts on the wheel! Tears of frustration, perhaps an expression of the fact that other things too are conspiring to be difficult just at the moment. I feel I should be able to see beyond them!

The sun is pouring into my room, another joyous day. A little sadly, I try to accept my particular life and its demands. J. is withdrawing for one reason and another, so I get the message that it's time to wind up our friendship. Very sadly, but if it must be....

I haven't been anywhere for two weeks Can't work properly through sheer saturation and a longing for activity and a change of scene, but my efforts are being thwarted. Someday I'll emerge from the monastery, God willing!

Courage to stand alone!

From reading Rilke's Requiem for a Friend (Paula Modersohn-Becker) I think that the energy which generates poetry comes from the sheer inability to capture perceptions properly in words. All that striving – and all one has constructed is a shadow.

"For somewhere there's an old hostility/ between our human life and greatest work." *(Rilke: Requiem.)*

I wish I had known his Requiem for Wolf Graf von Kalckreuth on those dark days last year when I toyed with his fate. What I learned so painfully and slowly was all there in Rilke's poem waiting to be read! But I was too young to understand it. How strange that then Rilke went over my head, who is now an intimate inner voice. And what distance between me and the man who had already absorbed this Rilke! How did we ever talk?!

CHAPTER 12
Intimations and Exasperations

———

*S*unday 20*th* *March 1976*

Crazy! Crazy life!

Afternoon light and a single daffodil out above growing in the late sun. The day has smelled of Spring, and all the streets of blossom and the warmth of Springs past. In Spring, whither turns the fancy?

May it not spoil or go grizzly this new thing in my life: my neighbour over the road who came calling suddenly last week and seems to be falling exuberantly in love! I was fixing my bike outside, unaware of being observed. He came, saw, and left, throwing his hat into the air outside with a whoop!

Intimations of remembered pain makes me determined to be very careful of my own skin. But presently I'm liking and enjoying K enormously. What timing! We went out to the Manor and in the evening picked herbs in a sunken garden by the sun-dial. Next day to London in his sports car with the lid off. I gritted my teeth as fields and village swept in a great flapping and blowing around my head. Checked out the Kokoschka exhibition; some I particularly love. Then Idomeneo at the Coliseum.

I'm not making any judgements. If this is the current of life at the moment, I want to be swept in! But when it turns, may there be a graceful end.

At the time of this relationship, I was an au pair to the baby of an LMH tutor, a role which I held for most of my time in Oxford from this period. I adored the little creature, and later cared also for her brother and moved in with the family.

I took my little charge across to his flat yesterday. He picked her up with one hand and held her on top of him and she laughed and laughed – a tiny yellow worm on a great brown bed. It was a gorgeous picture! And as I held her and kissed the top of her furry head, mine was very tenderly kissed. Beautiful sensation!

Monday 22nd March 1976

Wondering. Oh, go carefully girl! The beginning of a relationship is so fantastiche – such a shame the wonderful amazement and fragility wears off so soon and little rocks and pebbles occur, against which one can stumble.

I can't assess my feelings towards K, the contradictions, where it might lead. There are times when it seems like love, total unquestioning, and times when I feel criticism, even distaste. There is much to 'accept'; tough morsels to swallow! And fear. We have touched on large issues; is it too soon? Time tells.

"Tread softly, that the blind mole / may not hear even a footfall" *(The Tempest)*

Wednesday 24th March 1976

No, no! I think we are too different. I <u>will not </u>be another onion in the string!

I had been utterly horrified to be presented with another woman, casually picked up, and invited in to share our evening. Whereupon I had gathered my belongings and fled back over the road in outrage and distress. Next morning early, a voice outside my window called me for a walk in the Parks. We sort of patched things up, which was necessary because we had a very imminent booking to go to Morocco with another friend of his.

Saturday 26th March 1976

Well, it has settled into something quiet and we are off to Morocco on Thursday. All I can do, I think, is keep an open mind and live in total present. It is all an enormous gamble, emotionally, financially and scholastically (I'll do no work this vac!) Yet I feel it must be, and I pray the future looks after itself.

I wonder how things stand between us. We don't talk much now, certainly not of emotional questions; don't seem to laugh much or share common thoughts even. Just are together. Am I really his type? All those bikini-clad and sexy young ladies he fancies! My way is very different. Is he my type? Certainly not the great wizard; just a perceptive, amusing and convivial companion. With him perhaps, I am the wizard.

Today we went out to the manor again. A warm grey Spring wind swept through the daffodils and rosemary. We sat side by side reading about Morocco, as glimpses of sun, the sound of a bird and the cooing of doves came in through the leaded windows. It was calm, civilized, and I felt greatly at peace.

Thursday 15 April 1976 End of Moroccan Expedition.

Oh, so superb to slip into one's own sheets, own comforts and possessions, even own company. And a long semi-practical, semi-symbolic bath of whole person to wash the Saharan dust from my hair, and the syndrome and sadnesses from my mind.

Morocco has been magnificent. Yesterday the Sahara; today the far north; then England and Oxford. Ended on an apt note. On the train journey to Oxford, I tried to sort out the pain. It is sheer incompatibility. Perhaps I could love him, and yet it would be impossible. There is nothing to do but to end it and remove those emotions already grown in those areas where they could take root.

Good to get back to my own life among things suddenly firm again after all that slippery, changeable landscape of the Moroccan experience. Things in perspective again. I was in such a vulnerable position on that trip, but now I see clearly that the things I found disagreeable were indeed disagreeable and unpleasant, and my reactions were right. I just didn't trust or articulate them. I have never loathed anyone as much as I loathed K at moments on our trip. Yet the same incidents reviewed in another light at a later moment are totally transformed. Something very odd going on.

But I've had enough of this sort of emotional turmoil. Returning alone on the train to Oxford I knew very clearly that it must stop.

Morocco

It was so rich. The high tension: moments of fantastic pain and beauty rasping together.

Marrakesh, that evocative word. First hints of unhappiness on the night bus to Marrakesh. A huge sickle moon hung over round

LUCY OLIVER

black hills, a strange exotic landscape with occasional palm-trees outlined. It was Africa; an exotic world; a new world for me. But I felt then all communication between K and me finally leaving. We travelled through the night and beside me sat a man heavy as a railway track, and we were on separate ones. I felt that breaking distance inside, a premonition of what was to come, the rubble of a relationship. The bus moved relentlessly to Marrakesh, and I foresaw what might lie behind for me.

From our hotel balcony we could view the feverish activity of the square and Souk – fire-eaters, snake charmers, musicians, each surrounded by a group of eager-eyed watchers, dirty, ragged and crippled. Next day we wandered through the Souk. Sun dappled through the vines into the dark crowded alleys. It was as if colour was concentrated in darkness, and being bartered. The feel of rough cloth brushing past; muddy donkeys with loads of grass slung across their backs bearing men with sticks, dappled too by the excluded sun. The boys jostled and bartered happily, but I sought a tiny heap of sun in the corner of a wall and would have laid down the body and mind which for some inexplicable reason, had suddenly lost the taste of life.

The trip to Casablanca ended badly, in a penthouse over the city with a new aquaintance, when the hashish appeared. I did try, but my body reacted violently, and I threw up all over the balcony. Travelling is a challenging situation, but even I did not understand such a violent reaction. I entered a state of weird confusion, Marrakesh become hellish and obnoxious, but yet so beautiful. I cannot explain. And Marrakesh is Marrakesh.

We carried on, and headed south through strings of dusty desert towns, leaving Marrakesh at dawn looking most exotically beautiful, for a spectacular journey over the High Atlas. S had his pack stolen at Tenhirir, when a hand entered through the low open window of a dingy hostelry and escaped before we could stop it. Retrieving the backpack was a saga involving agitated circuitous negotiations with the resident circus—ie. the town and its policemen. We got it back eventually to great relief.

At the Valley of Ourika, an evening round a fire at a small inn and good meal set us all purring. Began rolling kif and making music with a clear, wizened Berber host and two young boys who shyly joined in a beautiful demonstration of communication. K was delighted as we clapped and felt ourselves into the rhythms.

Next day the sun was not visible and it was drizzling rain. We reached Setti-Fatama and found a camping place high on a hillside opposite a Berber village, which turned out to be its cemetery! Unsure whether this was wise, it was also eerie seeing graves glimmering in the failing light as I gathered wood for the fire, wondering if we would indeed find a quick way down the mountain "with a knife in our backs". After a very cold but still merry roasting of our donkey-meat over a brief fire, we settled in the tents for a freezing, wet, utterly miserable night.

However, when we emerged stiff and chilled in the morning, it was a relief to see Spring and sun hit the valley with blossoms, green willows and waterfalls. K & S stripped off and showered under the falling water. Exuberance too far for me!

Later when we reached the Club Mediteranee, spread out like a castle on the desert sands, the prospect of a proper bed and bath was irresistible. I will remember morning and evening light on the desert, and the mountains rising all around from desert and dust, but the atmosphere of indolence and opulence and a deadening sexy charge in the place I found revolting. Arrogantly, I could not abide the combination of deadness and freneticism, and saw in it the bored culture of the uncultured.

Now back in Oxford, it's all fading—the glory of the Atlas, the high snow fields, the splendour of the mountain desert; rugged black outlines against a full moon on our final journey north. Colour is what remains with me. On the road to Erfoud in a taxi at sunset, an ethereal pink escarpment rose alone from the plain and glowed as if with its own light. Near at hand the rocks were intense with red and orange, more vivid and vibrant than I have ever seen. And of course, transient. On the other side, a long oasis was outlined against the setting sun, blackening the palm trees.

Thursday 29th April 1976

For crying out loud, where is my judgement? Why do I care about a waiting-list of Pretty Young Things to keep him happy and grace his dashing sports car? And yet I do! What sort of test is this, that I am failing miserably?

I do not somehow regret passion, nor wish that I was always in control and calm. Guess I'll never make a spiritual stalwart with such a philosophy! I wish to subordinate my will to some greater end, but what is this end?

This day, a day of Spring 1976, when the evening sun is full and calm, this is simply a day—not like any other, for no day is that—but one day in the great battle I would like to see won.

Oh Lucy, get yourself together!

Do you really want to have anything to do with such a man? He wanted to be entertained, not to work at loving. What is this longing for love—such that any object will do? The affair with K has upset and wounded, as he dropped into my life, but I must forget this brief time I have stepped into a role so many others can fulfil so much better. Is it pain, or simply pique?

Sunday 2nd May 1976

I think the foundation of my values and ideals needed a test. For example, K's criticism about not living in the present is totally justified. I am constantly comparing with the past, trying to accept it whilst being afraid it will rise up and strike me. Then extrapolating every present moment into the future, I'm afraid it will not come about as I wish.

Yet, neither is K's version of 'living in the present' right. It is blind at both ends: escape, by blotting out the past, and avoidance of the future consequences of present actions and responsibilities!

The ideal has to be something about fearlessness, and confidence in the values of greatness held by the few because others are not interested. It's far too easy to think that the values of the majority are what life's about.

"I think continually of

Those who were truly great...

Whose lovely ambition was that

Their lips...should tell of the Spirit...

Who wear at their hearts the fire's centre..." etc.

(Stephen Spender)

Tuesday 5th May 1976

I've set my life and judgement back on the rails. What wild error of fantasy led me to get mixed up with K! I guess I was ready for something outward, passionate, non-mental at the time. On what level could he and I even remotely communicate? Anyway, that is over, with brutal thoroughness.

And I'm back in my cell, in my inner life, which necessary though it be, has surely outlived its period as regent. I must wait, fight the awful impatience which wants to be out in the world loving, doing. Ah well! I feel a little despairing this evening, lonely and goalless, and it's too early to seek the oblivion of bed.

Monday 11th May 1976

Machinations yesterday, and last-minute cogitations when it was revealed that K would be at a picnic in the Parks which I was also due to attend with A and S. What ensued was an enjoyably strained non-speaking situation on a Summer Sunday by the river, watching K with a little band of women seated around him (2 tiers of them!) The men clung together for self-preservation around our group. K's new lady gyrated ostentatiously in pink gingham, and I got rather be-drunken and flirted with S, and was rolled around in the grass.

Sunday 16th May 1976

A victory once is not enough it seems. It has to be won over and over again. I view the whole K affair in context, then suddenly I encounter him, and a curtain descends, activating a witch's cauldron of undesirables.

Then I struggle to lift the curtain again, corner by corner, and scramble up the Tree to my perch where all is calm, clear, balanced, powerful and unpainful. Relinquishing pain always feels like a betrayal of humanity, but realistically, pain simply cripples the system.

Sunday 22nd May 1976

So mild an evening, utterly still and full of a leafy shadowy thickness as the light dims. I stood outside to let my headache evaporate into the moist air.

A last bird sang, clear and invisible. Lilac and yellow broom lent final colour under the streetlamps. Few cars, few people; a silent bicycle or two.

Me—North Oxford—summer night. Felt very present.

K came over today, and if there a connection it was so subterranean—yet I did feel it. It is so peculiar, and driving me crazy. The calm, warm affectionate sympathy I exuded today was exactly what I felt, but why can I not chop it off? Is it simply the constant re-seeing?

Sunday 30*th* May 1976

Grey and cool today. I've just been in the Middle Common Room reading Sunday papers which has a beneficial distancing effect by jostling together other people's lives and tragedies. The Review section can fit an entire life into one paragraph! By the time I've glanced through a few, my own life seems such a speck in the barrel it's not worth worrying about!

It's tranquil. Amazing how much sheer *time* is required for inner work. I'm not studying for my exams. They can look after themselves. This wrestling with the still uncontrolled forces of my being is what is important right now. I have learned a little to identify some of the wilder forces and passions which push me around so badly, and also learned to recognise what is constant, and to transmute one into the other and how to manage the process.

However, last night the furies got me again and I couldn't do anything about it. It seemed a *reasonable* sort of anguish! I was slightly tipsy, and fell into bed. This morning I awoke with clarity (and a headache). A post-mortem revealed what had been going on, but the storm had not affected a central peace— when I located it!

It was like coming home.

Yet time still hangs heavily. The other worlds work to a totally different time, but one has to live physically in the world of Time, our time.

DIARIES OF A YOUNG MYSTIC

The days are very long.

I fight impatience, knowing that only when ready will I be able to go into action. I am *almost* there, I think. Just a bit longer Girl!

I see it as being able to direct that which must be directed, not crippled by my personal awkwardness and anxiety into a riding a rudderless dinghy on the big sea of a situation. I turn my head frantically trying to see all the permutations, caught up and blind to everything not in my immediate field of vision, but if I take one step up, all is clear. Visibility in all directions!

But what a step! There is a parallel with the first moon-step!

Thursday 4th June 1976

How lovely is the interplay of art and nature! I see a tall green flower, unopened, spiring the evening against the dark background of the copper-beech across the road. The livid white car, a symbol in the darkening. It is framed in my window. The curtains are blue, and a bowl of roses releases its petals of crimson and pink to their falling. It is full of that intensity at the turning of nature and the light.

Dare I feel pain or sadness, or even joy, when all is so still and absolute?

Dare I impose my values, the writhing of my emotions, on such a scene?

No, I do not dare. I have learned peace, the strongest, most powerful, most difficult of attainments. Fragile yet, no doubt, but I have endured torments without pain today, in peace.

LUCY OLIVER

Monday 8th June 1976

These last days have been grim. Possibly compounded by cold and illness I felt at nadir of lowness. Exams this week; no work. Oxford life at an end.

I cannot live here much longer. It is too difficult to have to see K constantly. I must go away as soon as I am free. If I withstand specific instances, somehow cracks appear later, like a bridge when a lorry has passed over.

Strange days. When I look back, what will I see? Days of summer in Oxford, LMH ladies spread-eagled on lawns, socializing gaily and traditional. The Summer charade, lovely and fleeting. And my final and only Oxford exams, neglected, unimportant, a hurdle to be passed, as is each day! I feel like a dark cloud when all around is sun. I know it will pass.

Sunday 12th June 1976

Returned from walking in summer fields. My vision was very lucid, calm, and the whole lovely universe seemed to fall into place, its workings almost manifest. The sun was low on the blown grasses and reaped fields. I thought of the universe, of myself and life, and the understanding accomplished over the last weeks. I may be pushing back the curtain a little, but what a tiny part I am in a vast scheme!

Exams I have been enjoying them! Here's a surprise!

The ritual of arriving in the sunshine of a summer morning in Oxford, all in black sub-fusc, splashes of colour and roses in buttonholes. The formality; the tension.

As we gather, bells are ringing and the rest of Oxford life goes on. In the exam rooms all is civilised. Dons in red and furry hoods, dignified. Calm prevails as light enters the large windows. One scratches diligently for three hours. Somehow it all comes out and is entered diligently in the script book.

Then it is over. Gathering again, the relief and comparing, the champagne crowd outside Schools. All such an Occasion!

In between exams I wandered in the Botanic Gardens through flowers and perfumes, and ate my lunch to the sound of bells, cramming information into my brain and watching little birds of many denominations hopping from a Chinese bush to another from Malaya.

Oh, so nice! These exams will be most memorable, particularly if I pass, and it seems likely. Sad that it will soon be over. But I doubt that two more years of this delightful sheltered atmosphere will be the plan for me. I've laid a foundation of thought this year, and I guess the time will come to use it.

Thursday 17th June 1976

In these days I must consolidate. How can Truth of Being vanish behind a slice of bread and jam, or the advent of another person, or a slight chill in the atmosphere?

Then—kaboom—time rules again with a blind and iron fist, suitable for natural processes but not for super-natural.

But I must consolidate and grow stronger in stillness and solitude. I feel such a feeble baby of the spirit, hardly worthy of the grass of the field which has no pretensions!

Saturday 19*th* June 1976

Saturday morning, as so many, each with that particular 'Saturday' quality. Saturdays alone; Saturdays with friends; Saturdays with a man beloved.

This Saturday morning it is wet and I am alone. I think I don't want to describe inner matters but keep this diary as a river of the outward—but outwardly there is nothing: no plans, no inclinations.

One completed Diploma, one year come to an end, a new pattern about to emerge, but from where? From the Future...how very amazing! I have no intimations, so I wait and try to be ready.

Later I see it is raining again. All day water has poured from a faceless sky past the greenery outside my window, relentlessly. So, I stayed in and read and slept, and the hours passed.

With evening there came a break, so I set off to my 'Heath'. Wild as ever, wind and sky, fragrant and damp. Where would I be without some rampaging nature nearby to externalize the moods of the soul?

Sunday 20*th* June 1976

Memorable day cycling with N. By our return, tired and happy as the sun set, we had covered at least 25 miles. Magnificent achievement for me!

And the countryside positively shone, with great white clouds processing across summer fields, and villages thick with roses and thatch and perfumes. It was Midsummer Eve, and how very full of Summer, and the glee of speeding down hills with effortless speed. The countryside lay clear and many-greened until evening, when the distance grew blue and misty. Beer and Ploughman's supper in a pub.

Thus, we caught sunset on Midsummer Eve.

It felt very special, simple, spectacular, celestial showmanship of the highest order. We leant on our bikes for a long time, breathed the peace, and the violently beautiful yet serene dying sun on this longest day. Doves, black against the light, flying to roost in a great elm.

This year has reached a turning, and so also my life. Why was I born, but to stand on this ridge this eve of '76? What more can one ask? If I were able, just once, to fashion a tribute to the glory of life and its formations, to show forth the light of the world behind the worlds, then all would be worthwhile.

Sunday 26th June 1976

Aa momentous week. First of all, I passed the exams fairly well, and have the opportunity to continue. There was nothing feigned about my surprise and almost consternation when I discovered this! I had been so sure that whatever future options opened out, it would not be this!

But the direction is available, and I must take it unless something else manifests. Problems about topic of course. I can hardly conceive three more years at Oxford! When I decided that spiritual matters were more important than work these last three months, I knew it would take care of itself, but I was still surprised. I had deliberately remained calm in that knowledge, but I think if I had gone into a flap, I could be recuperating in the Warneford hospital right now!

On Thursday Glyn came to see me and gave me a meditation. It was an initiation, and it gives me joy. Irrevocably committed now, I feel I have a place in an old tradition, and have truly begun the journey. Whatever doubts and dark days may strike, I know what I am, who I am, where I must resolutely keep my steps directed.

I am very suspicious of joy, I realize. It seems like an indulgence, but there's no reason for not admitting a calm deep joy at the moment. When outward circumstances are propitious to inner peace, why not enjoy, acknowledge, even spread it!

I have outlined elsewhere more about my parallel life and study under the tutelage of a remarkable and wise man known as Glyn.

*See my book **Tessellations**. Meditation, under discipline, begins a process like no other.*

CHAPTER 13
Inner and Outer Journeying

———

A*t this point, with holidays to fill, I signed up on an expedition by
Landrover with some students enroute to Jordan. It was
organised on a shoestring. How we suffered for five interminable days
crawling through Europe at a snail's pace to save on fuel (30mph),
nine of us crammed together in the back, facing each other not the
scenery, with our backs to the windows. Countries came and went
unseen, backs and legs ached, and lunch seemed to consist mainly of
lettuce leaves (to save on food!). With enormous relief, I departed the
vehicle at Istanbul with another young woman, Kt.*

Saturday 7*th* August 1976 Istanbul

Gratefully Kt and I take to bed after a wonderful day. Istanbul is
all I hoped, full of the dirt and spices I associate with the romantic
East.

This evening as the sun set large, misty and red across the
Bosphorus and the massy pile and minarets of the mosque, we
stood on Galata Bridge. It felt fine to be there, in that ancient
city vibrant beside the water, with no traces of its bloody and
contentious history. Friendly people, a modern conglomeration of
the new and the old, which has been the fulcrum of empires. Loved
the souk streets this afternoon. It smelled like Morocco, and how
it all came back, but seems far behind now. The sacks of spices are
pungent on senses, not memory.

I cut my foot. Immediately helpers appeared brandishing a bottle of yellow liquid (detergent? peanut oil?) which was poured over my toes. Another person waved a large bandage. We have been so impressed with the Turks. After my expectations of a hard and savage race, these seem like the salt of the earth!

We gorged on baklava, peaches, Turkish Delight, all foaming with powdered sugar.

All this sensual indulgence is necessary compensation for the horrendous expedition of the last week! It seems extraordinary to look back—five days almost non-stop in conditions of excruciating discomfort. Lack of sleep, food, space; nine people behaving with admirable restraint and politeness! Quite an experience!

I enjoyed Yugoslavia—one and a half days down a long, arrow-straight road bordered by vast fields of sunflowers and maize—mile after mile after mile after mile...... But it was Slavic, not Europe as I know it, so fascinating.

When the magic of Istanbul fades, I must return to the brilliance, the sea and sky of Greece. For now, I have found a very compatible companion in Kt, so at last a holiday of the best sort.

Monday 9th August 1976

This was a very peculiar and significant day, well in the tradition of mysterious Sufi encounters. I had been given the name of a contact, L, and had arranged to meet up with him in the bazaar in the early evening. I wasn't sure exactly where, but figured I would find it following the directions I had been given on a scrappy bit of paper. The rest of the day I just explored as the fancy took me.

DIARIES OF A YOUNG MYSTIC

All day I have wandered through the Grand Bazaar of Istanbul, alone, unmolested, very happy.

Afternoon found me in the book bazaar, which was dappled by light from the vines overhead. There were other interesting little shops in this small section of the souk, but I was drawn by one bookshop in particular, stretching back into the shadows. I browsed the manuscripts and pictures displayed outside as if to buy, but of course had no idea of prices. Somehow, I found myself inside the dim interior of the shop, still browsing, and was greeted by a slim charming man with enough English to take my enquiries very seriously, and who politely sat me down to show me some wares.

In the front corner, a cluttered desk was presided over by a large man who was eating chocolate cake, which he immediately offered to me. Embarrassed, as I had already realised purchasing was out of my league and felt rather a fraud being there and being served so attentively, I accepted the cake, and ate it under the eye of the large man in the corner. With no language in common, he twinkled at me in an amused fashion, watching me eat. My embarrassment grew, and cake disposed of, I awkwardly rose to my feet, made some appreciative noises, and departed as quickly as I could.

I went back to the hotel, changed into a skirt and long-sleeved blouse in the interests of respectful modesty (not noticing that the front buttons of the blouse were somewhat straining over my bust and gaping when I moved), and set off to follow the instructions to meet up with my Sufi contact. I bought some grapes in a brown paper bag to take to the Sheik.

But hours later, I had tramped the bazaar from end to end, been jostled by tourists, climbed cobbled streets ringing with hammer-blows (the metal-workers street) and was sweating in frustration as the grapes burst out of their soggy bag. The instructions I had been given simply did not make sense! I had a little hand-drawn map, but I could not orientate it to the vibrant life around.

Finally, as my despair was at its peak, I traversed an alley-way, and found myself back unexpectedly in the book bazaar. At this point, like a slow tide rising to my throat, an awful realization started to dawn. There in front of me was the shop I had entered earlier in the afternoon. It had to be the goal of my search! And I had been there already!

If I had been embarrassed on my first visit, it was nothing to what I felt then, making a second appearance, late, hot and sweaty, exhausted, and clutching a disintegrating paper bag of grapes! These I presented to the man in the corner, the man who had given me the chocolate cake, whom I later knew to be the great Helveti Sheik, Muzaffer Ozak. He looked even more amused to see me. The grapes were carefully placed in a silver dish. Flowers stood on his desk, gold bindings on books shone through the dust; people sat quietly as L and others warmly displayed fine old manuscripts to customers. It was an atmosphere of absolute calm and beauty in the quiet vine-covered corner of the bazaar. Timeless.

When I left, holding a large heavy edition of the Koran and having been invited to come to a zikr on Thursday, I was quite ecstatic. The reality of it, the holiness seemed to follow me into the evening sunlight. Why am I tempted to waste my time in superficialities when such wordless depth exists?

Friday 13th August 1976

I shall always remember my last night in Istanbul. Dinner with L and his wife on their balcony overlooking the Bosphorus. So nice they were.

Then to the zikr. We lurched through the suburbs in a crowded bus, L and myself, and an American girl full of impressive talk about her own Sheik back in the USA. She looked totally the part, modestly covered from neck to toe in a long djellabah. I tried pulling the tight sleeves of my blouse down a bit further and hunched my chest so the buttons did not pop open, feeling like a gauche imposter in this 'proper' company.

Somewhere down a back street, we left the bus, knocked on a hidden door, and were led past a shadowy tomb through a small door behind. Men in long black gowns were gathering, and I saw the Sheik of my previous acquaintance to one side. The men began their circle, and the chant and stomp gained in speed and intensity, which was fascinating. My critical and ethnologically-trained brain didn't stop for a minute, as I strove to understand with the heart, a manifestation so unfamiliar. It was like a sophisticated version of African tribal dance. I understood, and yet did not understand. I think perhaps I never will be able quite to attain that sort of communion. I cannot 'abandon'—yet.

It was so good to be among people who *understand*. L seems the only person of real intelligence I have met on my travels; it is so rare. But it saddens me, and tonight I felt a little sad and alone, that with all these people in the world, there are fewer and fewer now with whom I can know real communication, and more and more with whom any communication seems impossible. But I must not dwell on this; part of the price, I guess.

Anyway, when the zikr was ended, the American girl was making full use of the chance to meet and tell others about her training and American Sheik, so that when L was ready to leave with us, she seemed totally unaware, and he had to wait patiently until she reluctantly dragged herself away. While waiting, Sheik Muzaffer beckoned me over and said something in Turkish. Looking me in the eye, he handed me a string of prayer beads made from olive pits. I thanked him awkwardly, and asked L what he had said. With an air of slight surprise, L translated:

"He said: 'You can come again.'"

I went away, hugging these words, said not to the 'perfect' visitor, but to the discomforted one with bursting buttons. I won't forget.

Many years later (1985) at a playgroup in the local hall with one of my small children, I met a mother who had Sufi connections. She told me Sheik Muzaffer had just died, and I felt a sense of loss, and also surprise that I should randomly meet someone who knew this.

Tuesday 17th August 1976 Samos

I hear a donkey braying on this enchanted isle, and the noise of the restless Aegean scraping at the pebbly beach. The night is clear and warm, the air filled with flowers; people sitting in the small white streets.

Greece has really been a revelation. I suddenly feel I understand the springs of our western mythology. The gods come alive, the richness and promise of all worldly beauty, an idyll realised on earth.

I walked into the hills this morning, among the pines, pencil cypress, olive trees, figs and vineyards. The small stony path seemed to drop with fruits and good things: berries, figs, grapes. The wind was cool, the sun hot, and in the distance, a blue sea and white village. I was thinking: this is the source and centre of our whole culture. It seemed to vibrate in the air. The island on which science was born: Pythagoras, Aristarchus. Somehow, I am not surprised.

I was glad to leave Turkey in the end, and felt a powerful urge to leave and to be alone. Kt and I suddenly parted in the middle of the Green Mosque at Bursa. I just said: "I'm not happy. I must go on to Greece", and was on the next bus. Rather strange how strong was my compulsion, and how free I felt being alone. Well, ostensibly alone: I have been adopted and cared for at every stage of the journey! But Kt and I had started to be a drag on each other.

I enjoyed my bus journeys through Turkey, watching the peasants working their fields etc. and was adopted by an old Turkish lady who clearly thought I shouldn't be travelling alone and shepherded me along at the stops and appointed herself my protector. But with great joy I have embraced Greece, and being alone, I've become more centred again.

I arrived after a rather spectacular boat-trip from Kusadasi. The evening sun was dancing on a sea which tossed our small craft like a cork. I sat on the bows and looked on Greece, rejoicing at the blue island shapes. Two hours later, considerably queasier, damper and cooler, I yet raised the energy to look with amaze as we turned into Samos harbour, with the sun hanging like a red ball at the end of the misty mountain peninsular. Round the quiet harbour, white houses. It was perfection! And the air smelt of jasmine in the steep, stepped streets.

Next day I landed in Kokkari in search of quiet. Immediately a miraculous train of events took care of me. I disembarked the bus and stood next to my little suitcase, wondering what to do next. It wasn't long before a large cheerful Greek man approached with offers to help as I obviously looked a little lost, and in my neat blue sun-dress I did not present as a shorts-wearing back-packer out for a riotous time! He seemed to know everyone, especially a friend with a room nearby ready to rent, and led me off at once. The building was undergoing renovation, but a delightful little room was just perfect. (Later, I realised the proprietor was inclined to be a bit too friendly, but I managed to discourage his interest.)

In the evening with Jannos, my new friend, his wife Lisa and two children, and another couple we set off to tour the island. It was the feast of 'Marias', and we joined the celebrations, parading arm in arm up and down the village street, followed by wine and dancing. My companions, especially Janni, are the most ebullient of ebullient Greeks—singing, dancing, laughing, shouting Athenians on holiday, who really know how to enjoy themselves.

Last night again we went to another village to eat deliciously under the vines with music and several slightly drunken men dancing. I am fascinated by all this lively jollity. My new friends have been so good to me and taken me under their wing, but I cannot speak, except in limping German to Jannos! My Greek is progressing *very* slowly.

But I am happy here, and will stay until the spirit moves me on. I feel I must develop a more disciplined existence if I do. I am becoming as fat as a Greek, eating far too much—though on no money! The old man downstairs has also taken a fancy to me and keeps supplying me with figs, yoghurt, grapes and mineral water.

Thursday 19th August 1976

My last night in Kokkari. The stars are full in the sky; warm and still is the air and sea. Jannos, Lisa and I, after eating souvlaki in the little square, walked beside the sea. It is strange—they are like old friends yet I cannot speak to them! Janni really appeals to me; I so wish I could understand what I think is wicked and witty humour. They are so full of contrasts, these two, a good lesson for one accustomed to boxing people.

I have loved it here, yet somehow could not enter fully into the beauty, and felt a little misplaced. Someday perhaps I shall return, and let the full beauty and peace wash over my senses. It is better, perhaps, to go to Athens now, but how I shall remember and regret this isle when I am back in Oxford! Place alone is not sufficient to create a full experience, but it has been valuable.

And these stars, which once Pythagoras and Aristarchus saw from here in this soft air, will shine all through the winter on the houses and donkeys of Greece when I am far away, wrapped in whatever life the fates outline for me in Oxford!

Saturday 20th August 1976

This evening, I saw Athens spread beneath me, misty white on the bare rocky hills. I am fascinated by the barrenness of the landscape of this fertile bed of culture. The Acropolis was beautiful, high above the city, a perfect temple to the gods.

Last night, after a long evening with a group of loud Italians, the boat finally left Samos. I was again looked after by a young Swiss. We slept on the deck, which was quite comfortable, and in the morning the sun sparkled across the sea and rocky islands. Coming into Athens, the spirit of the place reached me.

I am staying in the apartment of Jannos & Lisa, periodically deafened by the planes from the airport which take off just above the roof, and fill the windows as they pass. Madame Kathy 'grand-mere' is marvellous and has some French so we can speak. She is sage and sharp, but I miss the ebullient charm of Janni!

My last couple of days have passed pleasantly enough. I visited the museum and Gallery and returned in the evenings to Kalamaki, a bit reluctantly since arrangements for my slumber are somewhat makeshift. I sit mutely before an incomprehensible TV set until the old folk vacate the kitchen, and go to sleep to the fearsome roar of the overhead craft landing, it seems, almost on the roof of the house.

Friday 27th August 1976 Delphi

This must be *the* most classic romantic, cultural, historical, spiritual experience. I sat beneath Mt Parnassus and watched the sun set over the great gulf of Apollo, descending behind the gulf to the sea at Itea.

It is truly a sacred spot at Delphi. Birds sang beautifully above the ruined temple. From my high seat above it all, I watched a flock of white doves circling against the crags and over the grove of Apollo. Here in this cool, fragrant spot, I expected to see a figure with a lyre!

But just the tinkle of a goat-bell, a sound as of water, and the mountains deepening as the sun left them on its journey beneath.

I ignored the existence of tourists this morning, with their loud, uncomprehending bodies and voices. They must be allowed to crash blindly through the sacred spaces of the world—something might faintly penetrate! And so, this evening, just as I had wished, I was led up the mountain spur behind the town, and there lay for hours watching the light on the mountains of the ancient gods. Greece is without doubt deepening my understanding of our ancient heritage.

Saturday 28th August 1976 Perdika

The real Greece, but I'm rather too weary to appreciate it.

I've travelled all day, much of it fruitlessly, and with a listlessness born of satiation, upset stomach, fatigue and a longing for security and familiarity. Time to return to the old green isle of which I am thinking more and more lovingly. Home! Never has England and Oxford meant so much to me.

And now I am residing in a white-washed room in a white-washed village. A sickle moon hangs perfectly over the water and craggy shapes of neighbouring islands. Smell of souvlaki—sound of voices and plates carrying on the air from each vine-covered family meal.

Peaceful. Beautiful.

By the sea a squad of fat Germans have descended to eat fried squid in the restaurants. Feeling a bit low, I decided to bypass the octopus and hope for better things tomorrow.

Sunday 5th September 1976 Oxford

Never has a home-coming brought so much joy! I was simply very happy to return on a quiet Saturday evening. It is crisp and Autumnal, and smelling of England.

I began the long coach journey home by leaving Athens in hot sun, its bare hills and land lifeless under the heat. I thought of England and tried to imagine it. When we stopped for a break at a roadside restaurant, and I scraped in my purse for some money to buy a snack, I realized with a shock that I just had enough funds left for my bus fare from London to Oxford. So, no snack. Back in the coach, I felt some panic arising at my financial state, both for the remainder of the journey and for the unknown future when I returned, because I had overdrawn my account for this holiday and borrowed from the College. As I looked out the window, I heard a voice—in my head. It said: 'you know you need never worry about money', or words to that effect. I was startled, as I've never had such a clear inner locution before, but it was exactly like a voice speaking words, not my own, out of nowhere. It also came with a sensation of peace, and I knew it must be so. A proof came when I arrived back.

With Yugoslavia came the first breath of old Europe, and I felt I was entering my proper environment. The greenness, lush fields and woods, and density of the landscape. I very much like Yugoslavia.

This was a long day, but late that night we reached Padua and stopped at a hotel down the deserted arcaded streets of this lovely and familiar town. Strangely I was delighted to be in Italy, and it seemed odd to be there so unexpectedly. Milano next morning was extremely appealing, and I half wanted to get off the coach.

A beautiful drive through Alpine Italy, and in the afternoon, Mt Blanc. As I saw the clouds swirling off its high peak like smoke, I rejoiced again that such beauty exists. Mountains are so deeply symbolic, and this power is everywhere recognised. Why *are* they more 'beautiful' than a factory-yard?

We dined in Switzerland and breakfasted in France. Finally made the ferry, and there before me lay the object of my longing—England. It felt really beloved. The sight of my room, spotless, calm, ordered and rich with associations, re-created all the sensations and wonder of such good fortune.

This morning Autumn lay in the streets, moved like mist through the still leafy trees, and rendered all golden and so peaceful. Perfection. Strangely, Autumn in Oxford has for me nothing but lovely and positive associations, having always produced the beginnings of a new life, real or transient. May again new life come from the dying season.

I seem to have learned a great deal this holiday; for the first time maintaining a constant perspective. Despite small ups and downs, I carried always with me a deep peace and surety into the places and circumstances in which I found myself. Unity visible in multiplicity. Now I'm home I can establish properly a routine for meditation, and at the moment this seems more important than people or activity.

No word on the grant issue *(needed to enable me to continue studying.)* I am not worried. That which must be, will be, whichever direction it be. But I'd certainly like to know!

And today I discovered that somehow, inexplicably, £70 has appeared in my bank account, and has been there for some time, so I was not overdrawn at all! It covers, almost exactly, my debts to college. Yet still I have moments of anxiety about practical matters like finance and my career! Foolish girl; ye of little faith!

CHAPTER 14
The Landscape of the Intangible

A n unusually long gap of nearly two months, and the next entries are a little obscure to me now, looking back. I seem to be wrestling with some internal changes, and declare this in the first entry following a heading: 'In the beginning......'. There is very little daily detail of my activities during this period.

However, I began my D.Phil research, having received the necessary grants, and continued a social life whilst pursuing the metaphysical via my contacts, as well as reading as deeply as I could. I also began hosting a Kabbalah meeting in my flat about this time, with the two teachers Warren and Glyn alternating to guide the group. By then, I was sure that getting a grip on direct experience and coherent esoteric teaching was the key to understanding the spiritual roots and intuitions in myself, as well as in the archaic literature of ancient Zoroastrianism, which I had taken as my thesis subject.

My book **Tessellations: Patterns of Life and Death in the Company of a Master** is a record of some of the background training initiated at this point, as well as a portrait of the inspiration and wisdom of a man who escaped all categorization and who truly exemplified a different order of Being.

As I delved deeper and the ground shifted, there are few external descriptions over the next few months. I used the diaries as a sort of internal self-tutorial, monitoring the currents of the past as they *intersected with the present and trying to find what I saw as the still point of Knowledge. The word 'Knowledge' has a specialist sense in this context. It refers to perception of a different order/nature from ideas, opinion and emotions, and is the result of a developmental process, not the accumulation of information. The principles I was studying and practising don't appear in the diaries, nor the people I began to connect with. I noted only how the flotsam and jetsam of my own moods and states were affected and stabilised by the work of understanding in daily life, sometimes known as the 'Fourth Way'.*

What little I recorded over this period was a stage in a process. When you are in the midst of any stage, it is almost impossible to gauge its real truth and value. The road to realization/enlightenment is not a smooth progression, but is far more reminiscent of the ancient jalopies beloved by my father—prone to fits and starts, and often breaking down, particularly on hills! And sometimes you just can't fix a problem yourself.

(An aside: my poor mother had to finish her journey on foot to the hospital for my birth in her dressing-gown, when the 'Old Jewett', a 30-year-old automobile from the 1920's broke down on the way. She made it in time.)

Monday 25th October 1976

In the beginning.....

This writing has changed as I have changed these months. There is much to consider, which comes and goes through my mind, and scrawls itself across loose sheets of paper in great candle-lit handwriting—ideas falling into one another.

Currently the foul fiends are on the attack! I have moments of sheer anguish at my helplessness, my ignominy in the face of difficulty, my weak 'heapish' collapses into grovelling despair and frustration.

However, just in this moment—equilibrium!

I know in myself the drawing back of fearfulness, of a kingdom lost by a stumble. I look for the sort of strength which is not wilfulness or pride, and is not buttressed by feeble efforts and comforting 'beliefs'. Knowledge has its own and proper dynamism. I must let the work be deep, like a powerful original current in which my personal goods and chattels of life—will, intentions, hopes, fears, doubts, personalities—are drawn along in its wake like the tail of a comet.

I'm sure that at some level, real inner development occurs of itself, without conscious scrutiny. I just come along afterwards like a simpleton in a forest, exclaiming over the fascinations I find! I must set the controls with effort, but then leave off analysing!

I had a dream two nights ago: a great black ship, slim as an arrow, which continually essayed the land. It sped from the sea again and again, onto the land where it did not belong. A feeling of horror and fear. Am I essaying too much?

It is Autumn. So very Autumn, and the streets smell of the inside of country churches. Has someone somewhere opened a door? Or does Autumn hang perpetually within country churches, generated by decaying wood and the leaves of books whose summer has forever left, their illumination gone. When the Sun leaves even a body of knowledge, its shell is a crypt, damp and earthbound, where even the Moon walks strangely.

If England in Autumn smells of mute churches, isn't it a blessing that an English summer still smells of flowers?

Sunday 5th December 1976

"The brief sun flames the ice" *(TS.Eliot)*, and briefly also my room, before it sinks into an early immolation behind the copper beech opposite, generating an intense focus of light in the branches.

Briefness is the quality of these last few days, thick and white with heavy frost. The pond is frozen; small boys 'boing' ice across its surface, and the sun is pale and warm on one's back. It is at least beautiful weather, very Yuletide. S and I walked in the Parks this morning and now she is off to London. Again, everyone leaving, and again, here I am still!

But I hope not such a prey for despondency as of yore. All phenomena change, people, weather etc., but offset by the briefness around, I cultivate that 'other country' which is timeless.

Why does one forget so easily, and a veil fall so thickly on the mind that one could forget again—forever? Lifting and falling, lifting and falling, until perhaps it stays up longer, or becomes thinner with each effort. For example, I go to a party, and for the duration of it the party alone seems real and alive. I must raise the curtain in even 'thick' situations, even briefly.

At other times, alone, it is not so difficult. Yet I feel a vague longing for distractions, their warmth and forgetfulness, even when in a God-given situation of peace and 'thinness'! Remembering is harder in a busy, active life.

DIARIES OF A YOUNG MYSTIC

Monday 27th December 1976

Christmas in Hampshire with Sh and D was icy cold with frost, and on Christmas day the sun was brilliant on the barns, on the ducks and hens in their frozen yard, and on the illustrious authoress's house which was our abode (*Jane Austen*), and its grounds and church.

Sh and I went for a walk, and healthy fresh air obtained, we passed the afternoon by the fire cracking nuts and sipping muscat. After a careful experimental roasting of the chestnuts we had gathered, the first mouthfuls were spat violently into the fire! No doubt our antipodean heritage was responsible for the mistaken belief that any chestnut is just a chestnut. I was certainly ignorant of the fact that some are nice and sweet, but some extremely horse!

We sat, Sh and I, in that large gracious room, and the sun shone into the fire, lit the dark wood panelling and the Christmas table, until slowly it moved—the light and the table went dead, the corners took on shadows, and the mellow light moved higher and higher up the wall. Still we sat, and watched the sun setting, emblazoned behind the lead of the windows, filling them. I felt a great peace that it should be so glowing on Christmas afternoon.

Then the Eating! The glories of our Christmas cake, white, snowman-ed, and set about with crimson berries. And the pudding, blue-flamed, until the brandy from the spoon also took fire and streaked across the table.

"I wonder who else has had flambéd-table for Xmas!" we wondered. Nice things to remember.

LUCY OLIVER

New Year's Eve 1976

The familiar rain and water noises in the flat deter me from going out to celebrate! And I'm glad to be in. It often seems pointless going out, yet there is learning from sensations, patterned emotions and reactions which I can now watch arising in given situations. Useful. Yet insight comes when these impressions have settled into new and beautiful channels and depths.

I keep thinking, though, that this inner preoccupation phase must pass or I will cease to contact the world, and this cannot be proper human evolution. Just a mountain-top for a time—then the market-place.

So, what then, at the end of another calendar year?

No wishing that next year will be different, better; or that 'something might happen'! I must let it simply unfold itself.

I have lost interest in watching the antics of a rag-doll, (*Me. A little sketch of a floppy doll accompanies this entry.*) wondering what the world's doing to her, how she reacts or fails to react to her environment. Also, I think she *is* no longer. She has lain down her limbs, untangled the strings, and begun listening to the faint stirring and flicker of an attentional life. Then she becomes able to animate from within, her limbs move again, and the strings will rot away.

So, at this New Year, this is what we have: A quickening!

After this, my diary entries are sparser. I gave more and more attention to meditation and spiritual exercises, and the emotional

222

forces previously tossing me about seemed too egocentric and limited to bother exploring in writing.

I was tending towards withdrawal and ascetism, and also attempting to articulate abstract states of mind and being which, in actual fact, I had only half-grasped at this stage.

Sunday 27th February 1977

A deliberately chosen isolation of the spirit is a heavy price, but it's a familiar strain in the lives I read about. I pick up Rilke, there it is.

Ah, Rilke—a whole life? Muss es sein? Es muss sein. You gave out many fruits from your isolation of spirit.

I returned this evening from an anthropology conference in Winsor Great Park on Ecstatic religion. It set my sensitivity strings quivering like a harp, and alone in my room it was not a pleasant sensation. I felt quite a fraud at the conference, surrounded by a forensic and aloof analysis of both rampant religion and irreligion, given that I am secretly allied to the subject of the conference!! I said nothing as the tumbrils rolled, and felt fraudulent.

My two worlds had begun seriously to clash: the academic and the experiential. The resulting inner conflict led me to years of intellectual insecurity, trying to avoid the common pitfalls of dogmatism and pious righteousness without losing my bearings in the challenging landscape of the intangible.

This conference also tested my new resolution towards an ascetic lifestyle, resisting a sexual attraction to one of my colleagues which I saw as an exercise of self-discipline, and re-direction of energy for 'higher purposes'. Not entirely wrong in principle, but needing to be worked through! I had declared war on the old Me.

The body is pulled by the strings of past and future, but I thought those days had passed. Will I ever lose the delight of a male hand, strong and full-formed; of a long thigh next to mine; of the sheer virility of certain male bodies? Muss es sein? Oh, hell!

No—come on—you know moods are clouds which pass so swiftly. Tomorrow there will be nothing left of it, and would you stake your foundation on a creation of air? Even this reasoning is craven resignation! What about the quest for peace and perfect accord?

'Baloney', I keep wanting to shout to myself. 'Feel the pulse, the life around, all unknowing, and what vividness it achieves.....!' But, the vividness of the rainbow is ultimately transient. You have chosen, and if aloneness is the price, pay it gracefully. Whining negates it all.

So may I sleep now at bed-time, peacefully, and be increased by the lessons of this last week and weekend, and be made whole, for painful are the divisions in me.

Monday 28th February 1977

Is it idiotic to go against the stream of life? Why, why? What if I am wrong? If they're all wrong, the others who have found the narrow path and taken it? What fools are they, am I?

Sometimes my doubts attain a complexity and multi-faceted non-life which would make all the stars cry out—if they were conscious—if anything is conscious—if I am conscious and it is not one huge conjuror's curtain...

What is the testing for? What if it is not a test? Is Life one long exam in a solitary room where there are not only no fellow sufferers, but no examiner!

Is this what life's all about: to clutch at a candy, suck it for all its worth, cry a bit, find another and suck away again.....

Why don't I do what *feels* good? Because next moment it will *feel* bad.

And so it goes, a shuttlecock in the winds. No, no. Every true organised model of the human psyche points to a centre of gravity, and an experience of inner space. Centres are still; still as a leaf in ice, or the fish waiting for another season.

I don't want to be running, running, as a half-awake person is, so I am facing, facing, and this seems as relentless as the running. I feel rather lost tonight. This moment feels as fragile and adrift as the petal from a high-flung rose.

So many images of lostness in the world, and they are all, these lost folk, so very *lost*!

That's enough, Whiner! Fold up. It's getting late at last, and you can take your long-familiar body into the foetal dark of nylon sheets.

Friday 4th March 1977

Spring again. It's always a surprise! Yet the daffodils are identical year after year, and the familiar scent is flowery, and non-bottleable. It's the smell of concentrated sunshine. (Sounds like a detergent!)

Detachment must mean everything, so that must mean not only desires, but also friends if necessary. I feel sad at the facing, but I am still cluttered by other people's expectations of me, and easy conformity to 'normal' behaviour. Spring sap is rising in the body. (Isn't it amazing how much of one is sheer plant!).

Something is firm. It's being assaulted, but is holding firm so far. These periods of vehement challenging are useful.

Visit from Greek Beau yesterday, who wanted to carry me off to Greece with "no half measures"! He's either a complete fraud, or most enigmatically romantic, in which case, I hope I was not too hard in my renunciation of his offer!

Sunday 6*th* March 1977

It has been such a strange week, as if inner psychic events have actually extrapolated themselves on to events. I have felt in the grip of inner adjustments as if possessed by an external force. Body shivers etc.

Everything this week has been a confrontation between phenomenal happenings and real convictions. I think what has caused most distress this week was a feeling that perhaps there are no longer any real grounds for friendship between S and me. Suddenly the total opposition of our fundamental attitudes presented itself and had to be faced. It's still an issue, and I'm not sure what to do, except there's no point in doing anything drastic.

Can you call 'friendship' a rather superficial matching of images and mutual pleasures? If not, is it worth maintaining?

Saturday 12th March 1977

Last day of term yet again—leavings—the warmth of a Spring afternoon. I remember this time last year and what events were preparing themselves to be born! With gratitude, for all things of the past now seem rich and strange, and so much part of the present that I feel like a fruit-cake composed of them.

No more money for this year or next I was informed by letter. I am almost glad not to be any more committed to something which still presents doubts—the Zoroastrian question. Frankly, I can't see me producing any great scholarly work! I'll try, if need be, but I doubt so much that I possess the equipment for academic endeavours. When I was in constant anthropological company this week, I realized again how unfitted I am by temperament or inclination to pursue the academic path. I find discussion of typical anthropological subjects tedious in the extreme.

I invited nine friends for drinks on Thursday, and the gathering immediately polarized into the Anthropos and the Others, and I knew which half I felt most in sympathy with! Problems then!?

Today I am doing what alone seems worthwhile, reading about Rilke, Stravinsky etc. The covers of the books are so familiar, and I remember D. Only his example sustains me, the dedication, the self-discipline. I can't call it Love any more, but foundation.

Sunday 13th March 1977

The image of angels is coming to mean more and more to me. It is an image which expresses the inexpressible nature of the experiences I am dimly glimpsing, of complexity and inter-relatedness beyond my wildest imaginings. Rilke helps, for I think his language is that which mysticism must learn to speak for 20th century ears. I am daily amazed that such comprehension should exist, and is available for the groping understanding of one like me.

S came this morning. Events are beginning to hurl themselves at her, and I think she is breaking into the chaos which also holds enormous promise. I felt so inadequate, terrified of saying something which might close the door which is opening in a timid wind. At moments she has an honesty and clarity of self-vision which is sheer beauty. But the door will inevitably close again, and has to be opened perhaps many times, so aggressive is the grip of the ordinary world.

Dear World, but why are you so loud? Quiet voices have to express themselves in a momentary lull of traffic, as it were, but are quickly swept off into the ordinary tumult.

I wonder if I will be able to be creative with what I am perceiving? Inner knowledge can't be articulated until it has joined together, risen, and emerges cake-like in some digestible form. In writing this I want to pour out all kinds of fat, full things, but I can't, so they just weigh me down like a swagman with his pockets full of pilfered fruit!

I have my books, and the rain outside, and this quietness so intense. Being alone I have the space for possibilities. So alone. So quiet, but voices coming from noiseless pages find something within me to talk to, and it answers to them.

What is this inhabiting my too solid and sullied flesh? Me I know, the old-familiar I have known from a child. But something else has come; a soul perhaps? An inhabiting angel? Experience of the Guardian angel? Malkut? I sense it can talk with all things, in a continuous multilogue of essential voices talking to each other. We can listen in if we keep very still.

I'm getting very Rilkean, but if I talk his language just for a while, I might understand more.

Tuesday 15th March 1977

"Anticipate all farewells, as were they behind you

Now like the winter going past.

For through some winter you feel such wintriness bind you,

Your then out-wintering heart will always outlast." *(Rilke)*

Yes, these words are right for now, along with the warm night wind of March, and the constant tap and scattering of rain. It is necessary to say goodbye to the past, to parents and family; to the present, this room and the cushioning paraphernalia of an arrived life, friends; to the Spring which has not yet come, and the round colourless drop of the future–to be free, to be truly free and truly poor. All must be left. Watching, flattened against the windows of an ever-departing train, they fall behind.....

I think Rilke was Orpheus, or an instrument which plays by itself as the wind moves through it, unknowingly. It did not make itself. It was made, and acquiesced.

Thursday 17th March 1977

"Ah", he said, "when you start feeding birds It's a sign of lack in the love-life!" Glyn, on one of his visits, unexpected as ever!

However, I do feed them, a rich colony of the russet-breasted, blue-crested, and fat and tatty sparrows among the rocks and greenery outside my window. But they feed *me* also, and it's an unequal exchange!

As always after a visitation by Glyn, the world has grown so much, it will take days of quiet absorption to become familiar with its new outlines, and "suffer a sea-change into something rich and strange." I see it as leaving behind all conceptions, so the forms may grow of themselves around the force which calls them into being (Love), and without the limitation of expectation.

Thursday 24th March 1977

Returned from Suffolk. B and I drove up on a golden Saturday afternoon, talking so hard the five hours slipped past imperceptibly, as did most of the scenery!

It was a memorable weekend in the wild bracken and pine, criss-crossed by roman roads. Sunday was warm and bright with sunshine, and birds sang on the blossom without my window. We walked through tall lanes to P's little cottage, set like an oasis of daffodils and red-brick in rolling brown fields. It smelled of summer and peace.

The countryside generally seems to reek both of the past and an eternal future. B pointed out a blasted tree which once held a light facing to sea, and a tall cottage of tragic history which was a centre of the smuggling trade. But there is something about the lie of the fields which I can only describe as germinative; full of some potential, which may be the less 'tamed' character of the country.

I have a vivid memory of the oak-wood, all gnarled and golden in the sun and tangled with bracken beneath. And still. Full of life, but totally still. We basked behind a gorse-bush watching the blue sky and dark movement of pine-forest at the cross-roads of Roman civilization, and there came before us the symbol of another crossroad in history: what Christ may have been in terms of world development. 'Cross' was somehow emblazoned into my consciousness with an insight.

Then we went gathering mussels across the mud-flats in wellingtons. The wind whipped B's blonde hair, scarf and green dress against her pregnant form as she bent single-mindedly culling in the rocks. Behind, the low sun streaked across shining mud. A small clump of coloured boats on the cliff against a dark sky.

As we returned, a lark sang above us, and a white barn-owl hunted low and silently over a pale field. Horses moved against the tree rims.

Next day, wet, we walked on the shingle beach; wild grey water, tearing wind, and a solitary figure approaching from the wind.

Constant sound of stones rolling against the waves, and a row of bleached cottages fronting the wilderness.

Mussels for lunch—delicious! I like B's parents and their pretty house: white doves, gables, dogs and daffodils.

Thursday 31st March 1977

I am trying to free my mind from accumulated representation of other times, places, experiences, cultures. I draw on so many varied sources, and each colours my thought-forms when it is ascendant, ie. Tibetan Buddhism, Yogism, Rilkeanism, Medieval Kabbalism, Zoroastrianism, Blake-ism (of the last couple of days!).

It's an interesting historical situation to be able to absorb so many approaches to expanding consciousness, but dangerous too, is the picture of reality forged from such disparate ingredients.

Writing things out turns thoughts into butterflies skewered on a pin, lifeless and incapable of growth or movement of subtleties (ie. everything I've written above!!) Thinking is straight-line, whereas images or symbols contain multi-dimensional potential even when written. I worry about writing. It's all I can do, but it seems to become increasingly impossible. How can one communicate anything? In the past when an individual tried to express the inexpressible, he did not face a bankrupt workshop as we do today: there was a shared language, standard symbolic forms, tradition.

Why am I writing these things out? Who am I trying to convince?

In silence fruit grows, and suddenly it is. The forces of generation come from all directions, inner and outer, and bear upon it, unobserved. If I cultivate silence in the heart, silence in the expanses of the mind, then perhaps something will come to be, of itself?

Tuesday 19th April 1977

Life itself is a work of art. I renounced poetry years ago. Just at the moment of stepping off the kerb to cross the North Circular Road, I resolved in grandiose fashion to choose Life rather than Words. But I remember it so clearly because it was one of those casually potent perceptions which condition the future. But of course, I didn't have a clue what I meant by it!

Spring, warm and still. The quietness of life at present is a great contentment, and all the people and places and preoccupations of the past seem to have slipped away.

Perhaps I dreamed it all—my whole life—while sleeping in the sun, and only that which is *recognised* will remain. It does seem that everything which is not essential, ie. of my most essential nature, becomes past, fast!

Saturday 16th July 1977

"If thou wilt know the invisible, have an open eye to the visible."

"Speak, Lord, for thy servant heareth."

Monday 22nd August 1977

I am irritated by the modern standard of poetry. Is it any more meaningful than comparing one thing with something else, no matter how inventively or originally these two items are juxtaposed? So what? Literature as a barren landscape composed of gnarled metaphors and similes, but bypassing essence, the thing-in-itself, and any significance reaching beyond itself.

I want to love the earth and its cargoes, but not just for itself, but because it might be part of Love returning to source. We move in love like rainbow fish in a coral reef, unknowingly. What happens when Source is acknowledged?

Tuesday 23rd August 1977

I have set myself a purpose, and that purpose is Freedom.

The freedom of the Desert, starkness and emptiness, is an image of the final reaches of the spirit. It's an archetype of ultimate freedom "....the desert's where I'm free...."

But Freedom is just the beginning; the first beginning, "into the first world...."

Looking back at this resolute intent, I am reminded of the adage: "Be careful what you wish for". The pursuit of desert and emptiness, of nothingness, absence of self, and renunciation of pretty much everything, can be seductive. It is not the ultimate aim of inner work, but a necessary transit, a re-alignment of values and energy.

Sunday 28th August 1977

Today every small thing seems laden with significance, vibrant with its own meaning. In LMH gardens, birds and insects are enacting the airborne battle of a summer's day in translucent blue skies under a rich, utterly tranquil sun. This morning North Oxford unfolded its berceuse at A's, with Sunday papers at the windows open to sun and ivy. My 'within' felt somehow liberated from its incoherence and mute questing, and almost present.

I regretted staying last night. Felt it was from weakness not strength, and I rose in the night to sit downstairs by myself under a Peruvian blanket, to watch the grey dawn and listen to the voice of the world within. I realized that its voice is now so insistent, so vivid, that I can no longer live following the thrust of outward events and trying to make sense of them— mute, puzzled, searching. I *know* something, and must now conform to the dictates of the "strong brown god", the river within: commander, vivifier, the Theos force in me and in the world.

All my padding to be lost. If those who have called me 'friend' heretofore are surprised, and find such a life distasteful, difficult, too intense, they must be lost also. Sadly.

I want to serve with every breath, word and action. "All is sleep around". So very sound asleep. Wake up! Blow on any sparks, igniting each to each those flickers wherever they are found in the ranks of our great earth-bound army!

I returned to bed, and as morning came, the centre and source seemed to be found again. So, after all perhaps good has come: more awareness. Talked to A; not communication yet, but perhaps slightly useful. He is so hidden, so resolutely walled behind his mind and integrity. Yet I like being with him.

CHAPTER 15
The Meeting of the Waters

———

F riday 16th September 1977

I moved from my college flat to continue my role as au pair to the children of a college don, in lovely attic rooms overlooking the college, and with an original painting of roses by a well-known painter which I loved for the two years I lived there. I was writing less, pursuing my thesis researches, and simultaneously what I considered my real 'field-work': esoteric philosophy and practice, with weekly trips to London.

So, it's not to be, that silence and solitude I felt would enable the 'within' to mature and grow strong, but increased (semi-detached) contact. Moving next door is a challenge: to identify with another's family and life, and live in the midst of it! 'In' but not 'of', I guess.

However, the lessons of children are vital contacts. I am given everything, yet nothing is mine!

Christmas this year was a trip to Crete with one of my old Australian friends.

Sunday 18th December 1977 Crete

First breakfast outside the Taverna in warm sun. Bliss! Blue sea and sky and the first sensation of natural heat on face and hands for so long!

It is Sunday overlooking Agios Nikolaus against the wall of the hill church, under an almond tree. The ground is strewn with nut-cases (the vegetative kind, mercifully) and smelling of earth and herbs. There are cricket noises, sounds of dogs, chickens, voices from the valley and a view of the inland mountains with snowy tops. We slept after our arrival, and woke to a vision of sea and islands.

Wednesday 21st December 1977 Knossos

Wandering among the stones of a deserted Knossos, I marvelled at the brilliance, clarity and precision. Who were they, these people of serpents and earthquakes? The earth and the Mother destroyed them, though they seem so light a people, barely touching the surface of the heavy earth, but taking of its fineness, spirit and riches.

Yet they fell.

Christmas Day 1977

Glorious! A full moon set over the town and hills as I walked to Church, following a black clad woman up the silent shadowy street towards the sound of chanting.

SA and I exchanged presents on our balcony overlooking the scrubby island with its white church, and a ship on the sparkling sea, and then set off for the beach. We came to a large cove where the beach was rimmed with huge feathery reeds, silver and bending in the breeze, and behind it, the familiar eucalypts of home. Ahh! We tried to climb through rocky muddy terraces, but were driven back by a strident chorus of barking which announced the presence of some habitation on that seemingly so infertile red land.

However, it was a perfect little cove for us, tiny, warm and sheltered, looking out to sea and the ship. We soaked up sun all day on the pebbles, ate stale bread and cheese, oranges and pistachios, and sang Rogers and Hammerstein watching the water rippling in the rocks. A large crab traversed the beach, watching us warily, much the way we watched it!

In the afternoon, we saw The Birds! In perfect harmony, great circles, streamers and spirals appeared in the sky. It became one Bird, the Great Bird, who flew and played with the sky, roaring with a thousand wings, turning, joining, separating until it vanished into the silver reeds. Then came a deep terrifying twittering from its thousand-throat, invisibly, as the sun sank low and the feathery tops of the grasses stood still and open.

Tuesday 27th December 1977 Elounda

An experience of huddled villages, turkey-cocks, animals, cobbled roads leading through olive trees, and of light in small courtyards, pots, heaps of sticks and wood, and remnants of vines clinging. By rocky paths we climbed the hillside to admire the windmills at the top, huge wooden wheels and cogs, worm-studded. They were old rough and beautiful.

We were invited into a small café, and took our place with lined Cretan faces round a grubby table. The host moved quickly to provide small chunks of veal, beer and hot potatoes baked on the iron stove. Around it clustered an old gentleman in scarf, boots and brilliant blue of eye, and a large woman who was feeding children with mounds of rice. It was hospitality of blue eyes and wrinkles, much laughter, and a childlike exchange of languages.

The valley was green and paradisical, touched with the silver-grey of olives, as we climbed higher to gaze on the sea and knobby islands of Greece. It was a panoply of water, land and light, very elemental, and no refinements on this basic theme. To the right of the blue, blue sea, the Cretan mountains rose high, rugged and bathed in a blue haze with streaks of sun.

Scrambling among pungent herbs and mud, we descended to be conducted along an invisible path by a brown man who left his olive-gathering and put on his coat from where it hung on a tree. All the way we sustained a true sensual assault of earth and herbs, along with spiced smoke from within the walls of the villages.

We managed to get a lift back to Agios swaying in the rear of a small truck, which was quite exhilarating, the mountains darkening round us, and the sea flattening beneath.

Wednesday 28th December 1977

Alone, in utter timelessness and tranquillity, I walked quietly up through the vineyards into the valley on my way to Arhanes. Smoke rising, and the sound of donkeys as they and their riders picked their way down rocky paths. The tall scrubby range of mountains behind were sacred to the Minoans, and I came across a small church surrounded by Autumn trees. In Arhanes, as evening fell, the Turkish streets were a bustle of dignified trade, selling from small doorways and blacksmiths.

Friday 30th December 1977

On our final Friday morning we walked to Lato through olive groves and oranges, and ate lunch on the daisied grass of some ancient house, gazing at the magnificent bare peaks of the great mountainous island. What a powerful place is Kazantzakis' Crete, I thought. No wonder it produced such a heroic writer. We browsed for a long time to the bells of sheep and goats and braying of donkeys in this ruined town in its extraordinary elevated location.

Later, waiting for the bus home, we sat in the taverna at Kritsa eating yoghurt with rich honey like caramel, surveying women on donkeys, and men in wound head-cloths and boots returning from the fields at evening laden with olives, all making their way up the steep streets. We waited and waited for the bus. It finally arrived, but proceeded in a leisurely fashion to stop at every olive grove en route! We despaired of reaching Agios and our final meal at the Trala!

Saturday 31st December 1977 Iraklion and Kazantzakis

Joy! All flights from Iraklion were delayed by wind, so we could go into Iraklion in brilliant sunshine, and locate the Tomb of Kazantzakis isolated on its hill, surrounded by thorn bushes. All around lay the city in a tangle of buildings and television aerials and dusty streets, and the deep blue sea. A Greek man stood and mused with us for some time before the stark cross, and the words engraved:

"I hope for nothing; I fear nothing; I am free."

Perhaps he heard as did I, the echoes of that feisty, passionate spirit on this windy hill.

We walked down again through back streets and lanes, with evidence of the Turkish days in a pink house and small mosque, and the souk-like market street. Gorging on our final sticky cakes in the market, I felt that my picture of Kazantzakis' town had completed itself. All colourful Cretan life swilled there, fruit, meat, cheeses, ancient booted men just sitting to gaze at the busy flow, their faces gnarled with wrinkles seeping out and up from the corners of their eyes. So warm, eastern and full of life, I hated to leave all this vibrancy, this blue sea and sky, and space. Yet I know this 'space' can set limits to the spirit—how difficult to desire anything beyond it!

New Years Eve 1977 Athens

Our unexpected bonus, to see in the new Year in Athens! Gleefully we booked into a hotel in Kalamaki and ate a delicious meal. Then we walked up a street very familiar to me to visit Janni and Lisa. (*My friends from the holiday in Samos last year*) What surprise on their faces to open the door to me, and behind them a chaos of people, children, presents and wrapping paper! Loved to see them again, and sat around the table talking as much as possible in bits of languages, with New Year cakes heaped on the table, and delighting in Janni's plump mobile face. "Noch ein Kind" slept in the bedroom, which was a surprise, but Grand-mère has passed on. I left somewhat sadly.

In Plaka we wandered by moonlight through old streets and courtyards, under vines, jutting windows, shutters and tumbling balconies. The whitewashed steps, and doors set askew all looked magical, and Athens city twinkled at our feet. Above, the Acropolis, floodlit and still. At midnight bells rang, shouts and fireworks rose from all over the city, and standing in that noble place, we embraced each other and saw in 1978. Athens did seem noble, pure in its whiteness and bare hills.

The following morning the final leg of our journey was about to begin, and at noon we left all that openness and light. On the flight, I gazed at the lacy coastline, seas of clouds and glimpses of earth, and tried to sense the World. The Alps were more beautiful than I have ever seen, range on range of snowy crests and ridges, with small settlements clinging where they could. The kingdom of the world looked so fair, it pulled deeply at my emotions. And is it all a dream? It is, in its way. I must not be seduced.

Here I have returned to something damp and cramped. However, filled with the sights and sounds of the world-face, I am aware of the real possibility, not of mere receptivity, but of creation.

Long gaps in writing now as I pursued my D. Phil researches and other inner work, practised meditation and attended regular Friday night group meetings in London in Glyn's kitchen, which is where I met the man I eventually married. No mention of any of this in the diaries.

The next diary entry came a year after the last, the following Christmas, when I wrestled with existential issues in the austere and beautiful landscape of Scotland. That interlude was for me a stage for the meeting of the waters, a conflict of two powerful currents, in which the world and the spirit, God and Man, collide into turbulence, and a way of reconciliation has to be found.

Christmas and New Year 1978-9 Scotland

To have nothing even in the midst of the most powerful 'somethings' which could tug at anyone!

I think this was achieved a little as I sat in the conservatory and watched evening settle over the silent Loch. Ice formed on the windows, the valley to Achergavel darkened and closed off its mysteries, while a sickle new moon hung above the valley in an indigo sky.

'Not this, not this' I would repeat, and with each invocation, the world without shrank a little, and flattened into image, losing some of its power to demand its own reality. The image-forms around me all became equal, a swirling kaleidoscope, though rich and strange. And there was something else, ungraspable, but potent and far, far more real!

Not this...Not these hills, high, wild and lonely, with the tussocky grass, the sound of burns in the black peat, the sudden springing of deer against the hillside, and once a stag, outlined high against the sky.

Not the wind-howl and crunch of snow underfoot, and most perfect aloneness with only ranges of snowy mountains as vast and remote companions.

Not the purple and gold range which floated like a celestial city the day I stood on the summit of the world over Achergavel. I loved them, and loved outwards into the wind and spaces so there was no answering warmth of emotion in the heart. This, I think, is the best way, austere; the other kind of love is merely sentiment.

Not these! Not the walk back into a silent valley as the sun set behind banks of cloud at the end of a long shining river. I faced it, and drew in its last rays, red on the grass beneath, like a food. I grazed on a feeling of ancientness, as if I had waited for this moment all my life, to stand here on this spot and salute the ancient sun through many lives. And of course, it is so; that 'ancientness' is depth, the touching inward of the place from which time springs.

Then I wended my way down into the cottage, tucked with its two chimneys into the side of the hill. The dark valley was so still, the night roared with silence and stars, and there was the Man, *(recently met, with whom was a strong erotic charge)* come in from the fields with his heavy bag of tools, looking wild and strong with an apprehending and quizzical gleam in his eye. Yes, I could have stayed on there, in that almost perfect cottage and valley, and he certainly called to the blood and the emotions! He set them all singing round my ears with longing for the old zing of the heart, and for a role, a place in the world.

But not enough. I was rescued from entanglement in the reins, from a net of powerful instincts more by circumstances than will, like a heavy bird escaping the ropes of a snare, and trying to fly again. This image is no weak casual metaphor; it is exactly so. Flight is not possible while bound by the chains of earth. If flight is possible, it must be done, so the world can be seen in totality.

Not these. Not my friends' little cottage, pretty babes, the warm womb of a lovely life and good pursuits, and the difficulty of seeing above entanglements.

Not the black sky and brilliant stars of New Year's Eve, and Orion bestriding the loch. What are these stars? Not of our world, they are the tips of other worlds, other perspectives, whole other times, which make our way of seeing and the cosy contours of our small mundane realities like the scrabbling of a mole in its hole, or the self-absorption of a child in the nursery playing with toys.

Not the world gone white, thick with snow, mountain-tops lost in the grey sky. Grey and white, depth and distance are reduced by the uniform mitigation of snow. Gambolling on a beach, clambering on rocks and seaweed, and sitting huddled in the middle of the Loch on an island. The air was full of flakes, splattering on my hood. Cold, bitter and unrelenting in its lack of human-ness is Weather, but joyous too, the joy of forces greater than human contractile being.

Not the day we drove to a volcanic valley, a quiet ruin, the cattle outlined beside the sparkling sea, and the air corrosive with cold, freezing the sun. We had to return to the car, defeated for the first time by the weather in its extraordinary crystal deceptiveness. Wee R could hardly move in his space-suit, his soft cheeks red, with bright enquiring eyes and lovely helplessness. Skye, Rhum and Eigg floated in the brilliant blue sea, celestial, almost near enough to touch, crystalline.

Not even the drear walk up the side of the hills by the road, torn by wind, unbalanced by internal forces, and solitariness become loneliness. I crouched by the burn, trying to sort out these nothingnesses.

Not any of these things, nor the tall white house, friendly people, cherry brandy, whisky and Atholl Brose by the fire, and too-good meals. A glorious Christmas tree, inundated by presents on Christmas morning and the children scouting about. I wanted to be part of this conviviality, but I watched and watched. It seemed a gay confection, and will dissolve in time, like candy in water, as it has already dissolved.

Love. It was all to do with love, all the drawing out, the warmth that was there and beauty. But also the pain and longings, the withdrawn quality: are not these the classic signs of love, a heart dedicated and suffering because separated? Separated from what?

This phase was a desperate wrenching away from the warmth of human contact in pursuit of an ideal. At this stage of my maturing, it was an idea of an ideal. Not wrong, but not right either, this worship of emptiness. All spiritual literature proclaims the necessity of a self-emptying and turning away from the world and the preoccupations which trap and hold our attention. but it is a step, not a destination, and the real meaning of emptiness is inner, not outer. It is to do with attention, which is a power, perhaps the only one we can command.

At this time in my life, I was dutifully trying to clear the stage externally. I feel pity now, for my younger self, and this struggle, which continued until wise guidance and the kind of effort and group work which combats self-importance and illusory expectations began to condition my post-Oxford life.

A final few, very widely-spaced entries, saw the stimulus to write a journal finally wane.

Sunday 7th January 1979

Here, in the darkness where images fade,

"...the faith, and the love, and the hope are all in the waiting.

Wait without thought, for you are not ready for thought:

So the darkness shall be the light, and the stillness the dancing." (*T S Eliot*)

No use to indulge in misery, pain or hopelessness: these too must go. Is it only a mute consciousness which is left? Perhaps I had better try it! Although what was so real for me in the hills of Scotland remains, I have lost the emotional energy from those wild and passionate images. What is left feels like nothing.

This was my last Oxford entry. I moved to London to share a flat with my husband-to-be, who had shared the same esoteric and spiritual training, and with whom I felt a life partnership was fore-ordained.

Monday 29th October 1979 London

Late afternoon settles over London, over roofs and blind windows, distant trees and a bank of cloud, above which half a moon rides in the pale sky. The light dies in the plane tree in the corner window. It gets dark so quickly now. The summer seemed perpetual, though not so much a summer, as a mildness, a non-weather which was pleasant and continuing.

Now the winter approaches and it is like a beast awakening in its cave, the first threshing of his windy tail and a glint of icicles in his eye as he gathers to consciousness. And the harrowed masses button their overcoats and prepare to endure yet again the oppression which they do not understand, but accept because it has always been.

This strange world! I am preparing to leave it; bit by bit the knowledge takes hold that this is not my home. I remember a bright planet, and as there is no longer any small thing I want from this world, I wonder why I am here. I have loved her so much, this world, even as she laid her fingers over my eyes and drew me down caressingly whenever I caught the sound of a horn in some other space. She sought to turn my head and fill my ears with the old familiar melodies of earth.

I never lost sight of the 'bright planet', but for the next period of my life I was busy with children, domestic life, groups, meditation and study. The demands of inner and outer seem to compete for time and attention, but eventually I realized the world is where the work is.

However, I no longer wrote 'from the heart'.

Sometimes I wondered if it had died.

POSTSCRIPT 2024

In some earlier diaries I found words which seem relevant to the impulse which led me to turn my Oxford years into a book.

"The reality of old age has always cut across my youth when I consider it. As unbelievable that one can be suddenly old, is the realization that one is young. Both are startling, and perhaps both are gratuitous. One day soon I shall be old. Whereas now there is nothing but future—for I have done nothing—soon there will be only past.

But something in me resists despair. Despair is fear disguised." (L.O. aged 22)

At twenty-two I was young and pretty and full of energy with all my life ahead, but I liked to test the future by sending my imagination into the great unknown. I think I was trying to taste the effect of Time. Would I be the same person if everything around me had changed, all kinds of *experience* added to my sense of self, and a wrinkled, very different face still bearing my name, looking back at me in the mirror? The present is so real, seems so eternal; what would Time do to my being?

I wrote those words just before I set off to the other side of the world. I am still here, and the time of being Old has come. I no longer feel eternal, but although the past now has a long trail behind me, there isn't only 'past.' Not yet anyway. The future continues to be present, taking its dimension from that same sense of the 'gratuitous', the ungraspable, non-earned, which I had then.

Mysterious origins, mysterious destiny—it was, and is, an intuition of the essential core of being which is neither young nor old and which does not age with the body.

I now see that all the experiences I recorded were a process of trying to understand and grasp something of this nature, something intangible but none-the-less central. I explored personal relationships, thinking and learning without actually *understanding* what I was about. I was too young really to know, and hadn't yet enough experience to name or claim it—which is as it should be. Life itself makes it substantial and real. To claim too much too soon can be fatal to wisdom.

We wear our age and identity just like clothing, mere rags of personhood constituting a "tattered coat upon a stick" as Yeats expressed it, unless "soul clap its hands and sing" *(Sailing to Byzantium)*. I am sure that everything I was writing then, and more consciously in the years since, was and is an attempt to 'sing', and to resist despair. Perhaps our best weapon against despair and fear is to keep sight of the intangible within and without, and *never to cease doing so,* no matter how 'old and wise' I think myself, how much learning, or how many experiences I have accrued.

Ways and Means

The *impersonal* power concealed in the darkness of our origins is sensed as a veiled truth in religion or spirituality, and also encountered through art, science, and the breaking of intellectual or emotional boundaries in various fields. In childhood, it begins quietly, innocently, meditatively.

DIARIES OF A YOUNG MYSTIC

As a very young person, wandering by the foaming breakers of the restless Southern Ocean, buffeted by wind and crying gulls, I nurtured this sense. Just over the tall dunes was a lagoon, where the sound of the wind and sea suddenly ceased, and was replaced by a warm silence and the gentle lapping of water among reeds. On one occasion I found a tree-branch low over the water which would support my weight, and there I hung above the still surface and looked into the future, the unknown and unknowable tessellations of the path my feet would walk.

(I have described in my book *Tessellations* how a sense of pattern began to cohere for me. Tessellations are interlocking patterns.)

The veil is sometimes thinner in youth, which is why I remember the tree branch and the lagoon, and the way my mind wandered in an enchanted maze of immanence for what seemed like hours. The cosmos leant low and entered my space and I never forgot it.

Strange thing was, many times afterwards I sought out that branch for a repeat performance and never found it again. The water level varied with tides and the breaking of the bar, but what had a happened to the tree? It simply was not there. I searched wistfully every time I visited the locality, and even half a century later passing through, I automatically looked across the water to see if the ghost of a young girl reclined along a low-hung bough.

Mere glimpses, real but evanescent; they disappear like smoke on the wind of everyday emotional experience: happiness, grief, frustration etc. How can we hold on to such intimations or cohere them into a meaning structure to live by?

As I grew older, I looked for patterns, patterns revealing *principles*, those abstractions by which one can try to understand how the world works. You have to gather together the glimpses as they arise, and engage with them actively to see what has substance and potential for structure and development, against what is merely wishful thinking or fantasy.

I began with religion, absorbing the iconography, mythology, rituals and explanations of Christianity as handed down in my circumstances, and exploring other systems and beliefs as well. But then I moved on, because collective rites and doctrines do not automatically deliver to those who embrace them the experience or *knowing* of the founders, saints and sages. Individual developmental practices are needed, with coherent guidance and persistence. Empirical work, 'field-work' as I saw it, began to steady the emotional boat of my Oxford years, and produced whatever degree of present liberation I can maintain.

Eternity and Death

Increasingly now, many of those I have loved are slipping off the stage, leaving a gap where they had always been in my life. Once I would have found it surprising that most do so gracefully and peacefully, even those who have no interest in spirituality, no grand theories of the after-life, no visions, sense or conviction about what might come next. Even if the lead-up of illness is disruptive and painful, it seems that once the fight to maintain one's personal status quo and existence is finally relinquished, something else takes over. The 'something else' must be inbuilt in us, part of our genetic inheritance from Nature, and operate in the same way that leaves fall from the trees in Autumn. Leaves detach gently, perfectly, as wind touches their surface. It is their own wind, the wind of their passing; not before and not after that moment. To recognize this 'autumn leaf gene', and spare ourselves the anxieties of past and future, is skilful living and dying.

Mercifully, in extremis, Nature itself ushers us over the threshold.

I wrote also:

"Something new, eternal, has to be born from every love if it is to survive the pressures of contraction, wavering and cooling." (L.O, aged 22.)

With so little experience at that age, I wonder why I boldly assumed love was a portal to Eternity?

Many 'loves' are extremely transient by nature. However, they do accumulate over the course of a life, and make up a foundation for a particular quality and approach to living. Some innate survival sense impelled me, even in depression, to find little things to keep love alive: books, people, a patch of sun, the shine on a wooden stair. The giving of attention is what matters, and although gloom may not entirely be dispelled, at least it offers a foothold in the abyss.

But then there's Great Love, like a Spirit taking possession of the whole being, stimulating new life, new energy, new circumstances. 'Falling in love' releases powerful energies, and exactly like the 'gods' of old mythologies, the force of Expansion and its opposite Contraction are both unleashed together, in a sometimes turbulent and life-changing emotional arena.

I now see the years of the diaries as birth-pangs, the shadow of the Eternal falling across my very ordinary existence.

All the years since have been an evolution.

I will now close up these diaries, and consign the original notebooks back into their trunk.

POSTLUDE
A Meeting with Myself

―――

"I 'll tell you", she said...

"...but you will have to find ways to work at embedding all experience in your body, and in your mind and in your emotion—all three. If any of these three are under-represented, you won't know anything. Your thinking-mind can be a trickster, often an imposter; your emotions, a sea where it is difficult to find dry land; your body, either a neglected work-horse or an emperor whose reign ends in the grave.

But if you manage to bring them all to bear on the problem of living with intelligence and attention, you may climb the Tree of Life.

Knowledge comes first. You have to work through the branches of the Tree of Knowledge which have been well laid out for millennia. Identify the basic principles so you can avoid falling off. Be careful of apples—they may have a worm or send you to sleep for a hundred years. Listen carefully to any serpent you encounter but never obey until you have mastered it. Once you reached the top, you'll know what to do next".

By this time the whole canyon was ablaze with crimson, laced along its ridges with threads of gold, and a wind rose to shuffle the leaves of the sturdy pines. It was time to go, so we left together.

"Remember", she said as we left, "I am not alone, and a long line of others has preceded me, each adding the context of their Age and individual characters, but the universal Laws are unchanging. We just grasp them differently and call them esoteric*.

I knew a man once, a stocky figure, gruff and glorious at the same time, absolutely indefatigable in his labours to till any earth he found with potential to grow trees, and he said to me on his deathbed: 'Girl, you'll find out one day'.

I am one of those trees".

———

*A note on the meaning of **esoteric**

With the technological revolution it might seem that what was once meant by 'eso-teric' has become 'exo-teric' and now available to anyone at the touch of a screen—ancient texts, secret teachings, arcane practices, many now de-constructed, packaged with therapies and attractively priced. In fact, what is truly esoteric in the original sense, is exactly as it has always been—hidden in plain sight, available but unrecognised, unsought. Like tracking a bird on the wing, a lark in the meadow heard but not seen, or the flight of a phoenix, only those who are alert enough or prepared to put themselves into the right place at the right time, hear the call or follow it.

The etymology of esoteric is simply 'within', that which is inner, and needs certain skills to be uncovered. It characterizes a kind of first-hand knowledge and presence of being. When meditation methods reached the West like a tide in the twentieth century, flowing into dry corners where conventional religion had left empty furrows of collective customs, people realised they could help themselves to explore spiritual life through practices which were ancient and effective. So, once reserved practices rapidly became a popular wave and created a whole new religious landscape, along with other social tides.

The landscape has evolved new dogma, customs, comforting practices and community, but none of these, per se, further the truly esoteric, which is resistant to mass dissemination and usually transmitted from person to person, ie. 'orally', not on account of being complicated or hard to understand, but rather for the opposite reason. First principles, derived from digging down to the roots and fundamentals, are simple but effortful, and also powerful—sometimes too much so for comfort or self-guidance.

About the Author

After leaving Australia in 1972 , Lucy settled in Oxford and began an Ethnology diploma and three years D. Phil research in sacred symbolism and Zoroastrianism. Simultaneously she began esoteric studies and practice, and was a founder member of the Saros Foundation for the Perpetuation of Knowledge 1978-2001 and High Peak Meditation. Her first two books give details of this background. She teaches classic non-denominational meditation, and trained in a coaching method working with metaphor and symbol called Symbolic Encounters.

Read more at https://www.meaningbydesign.co.uk/.

Milton Keynes UK
Ingram Content Group UK Ltd.
UKHW010301110424
440949UK00004B/226